MARKETING STRATEGIES

THAT REALLY WORK!

INSIGHT PUBLISHING
Sevierville, Tennessee

10 9 8 7 6 5 4 3 2

Printed in the United States of America

ISBN-13: 978-1-60013-1912
ISBN-10: 1-60013-191-3

Published by...
Insight Publishing Company
647 Wall Street
Sevierville, Tennessee 37862

Table of Contents

A Message from the Publisher

During staff meetings at our company we discuss ways to grow and prosper. Inevitably, someone quips, "It's all about marketing!" We all laugh, knowing it's not *just* about marketing. We're constantly dealing with production issues, customer service, cash flow, and more. But we have to admit that without the marketing programs that bring us clients, we wouldn't have to worry about production, customer service, and cash flow. So, maybe it is *all about marketing!*

Regardless of what line of work you're in, you need to understand more about marketing, media, and public relations. And you need to learn fast! Your competition is gaining ground and using marketing techniques and programs that you haven't even considered.

You've made a great *first* decision by purchasing this dynamic book, *Marketing Strategies!* We reached out into the marketplace and found some of the top media, marketing, and public relations experts in America and asked them to share their most potent strategies. As you read these informational and inspirational interviews, you'll learn powerful ideas to help transform your business. You'll also learn how these professionals can help your business grow even more by inviting them to work one-on-one with your organization. We hope you'll take advantage of this unique opportunity.

Interviews Conducted by:

David E. Wright,
President, International Speakers Network

Chapter 1

Lea Strickland

David Wright (Wright)

Today we're talking with Lea A. Strickland, author, columnist, consultant, speaker, and thought leader on strategic and tactical business issues, founder and President/CEO of F.O.C.U.S. Resources, a national strategic business consulting practice based in the Research Triangle Park region of North Carolina. Ms. Strickland is author of the book, *Out of the Cubicle and Into Business* and has appeared in national print and radio media including Entrepreneur Magazine and Entrepreneur Magazine Radio. Lea is a nationally recognized expert in business strategy, performance, and processes. Her clients come from all industries: infotech, biotech, life science, entertainment, professional services (accounting, law, architecture), as well as manufacturing.

When people talk about you and your success as an entrepreneur, consultant, author, speaker, and business expert, they talk about how fast you have built your reputation and that of your company. How have you accomplished so much, so quickly?

Lea Strickland (Strickland)

In starting my business I learned that marketing is about content. People are looking for content from someone they are comfortable with. They need a comfort level with the person they are bringing in to work with their business, and in order to convey content you have to educate your market. To get your prospects to call, they have to be confident you can help; they have to know what you can do. I've been successful because I do what I refer to as "education marketing."

Wright

What is "education marketing"?

Strickland

Education marketing is engaging your target market by providing information they need and can use. The information is "the education" and is valuable to your market because it meets their market needs, their wants; it helps them clarify what they need to do. The marketing aspect is part of your giveaway; it is free to your prospects. Your marketing strategy is to make a meaningful connection with content. Your prospects learn your expertise before they invest in your services. They know you before you walk in the door.

Education marketing uses traditional elements such as advertising and press releases to call attention to content—articles, books, booklets, Web sites, speaking engagements, and seminars which bring your prospect further into the realm of becoming a paying customer. You use traditional tools to call attention to your content. You use a mix of the traditional and the non-traditional to get your prospects to focus on what you can do for them. You want prospects and customers to concentrate more on your articles, newsletters, books, and the content on your Web site. By getting them to read your content, listen to your audio clips, visit your Web site, they come to know you. When you become someone they know, they are comfortable with you and buy your services.

Wright

How do these elements come together?

Strickland

The elements come together based upon your specific objectives, strategy, and the resources you have available. Each organization must identify a specific, measurable objective and develop an understanding of where their prospects are— what are they reading, listening to, and what events they are attending. You have to know what you want the prospect to do: Are you trying to get long-term customers, are you trying to get people into a workshop? Are you trying to get them to buy books or ask you to speak at an event? What are you trying to get your audience to do?

Once you understand your objective, you have to be able to connect with your market and fulfill a need that they may or may not recognize. You want to get a core message, get your area of expertise out there, and you make that match to the market which you want to serve.

Wright

Is it like a shotgun method of marketing rather than a single bullet? Are you doing several things at one time?

Strickland

A shotgun sends a number of pellets at a generally targeted area. A single bullet is aimed at a specific target. This approach is more of a rapid-fire of many single bullets. You have your site set on a specific target and you repeatedly fire at that target. Not a one time shotgun blast but an on-going barrage of messages and content. How frequently you choose to fire and what caliber of bullets depends on what your organization is capable of doing at that point in time.

What is your budget? What is your objective, how much can you do yourself? How much can you afford to hire someone else to help you with it? You may start out with a shot gun blast to get that first push of content out and test various venues for effectiveness. As time goes by you will put more emphasis on the single bullets aimed and fired on target repeatedly. You are not trying to do a "hit or miss" type thing, or just throw something out there and hope that you are going to hit your market. You are going to try to find the opportunities to connect with a specific group you are trying to reach which needs what you are trying to provide.

Wright

Would you walk me through an example?

Strickland

The best example I can give is from my own experience starting my business. First let me provide some context for the example. I started my consulting firm in an area where I had no business contacts or community relationships. As an employee of other companies, I was entrenched in the day-to-day closed community of those companies—whether they were a start-up technology company, a business unit of a corporation, or something in between. So I started from ground zero on contacts and connections. I needed to get a foothold in the business community quickly and gain a solid reputation.

I definitely started with a shotgun approach and I fired at everything that moved! I accepted speaking engagements at community colleges, business groups, networking groups. I joined and volunteered at not-for-profit business associations. I set up meetings with key decision-makers and community/business leaders. I attended networking and social events. I was out gathering as much information on potential prospects and competitors as I could. I studied the ads, sponsorships, and news stories. I did every traditional tactic that I could afford to pursue.

What I found was traditional tools were effective only after I delivered content. When I spoke to a group or participated in a panel discussion—people got what I did and could do for them. Up to the time they experienced my expertise, any traditional marketing tool, like an ad, didn't make it through their mental filtering process—it just made them see a generic consulting firm saying "me too."

The light bulb moment (you know when you suddenly make the connection in your mind that says—this is what I should do) came after a colleague sent me an e-mail which was requesting article proposals on accounting issues for small businesses. I love to write and the topic was one I was qualified to write on, so I sat down wrote the article, the proposal, the outline, the summary and followed the submission process. A week later my first national article had been accepted and was being published with only one minor edit. The response to that article from prospects and from other media outlets was phenomenal. It was the catalyst for understanding the market and for developing the educational marketing approach.

I write. I speak. I discuss. I share. I provide content. Articles, workshops, seminars, events, Web site content, and every bullet is fired consciously toward the market segment looking for "how-to" from someone who knows how to build a business from ground zero and combines that with cross-functional knowledge and scalability (small business to huge international companies). My market knows me through my writing and speaking. They will pick up the phone or send an e-mail to ask a question. They attend the workshops. They refer other people. Based on content I have differentiated me and my business from the competition. My competitors have become some of my best referral sources!

Wright

Is this "niche marketing"?

Strickland

It's "niche marketing," but the niche is broader, or maybe I should say deeper than you think. By using content, the common threads weave through organizations and redefine the "niche" to be something other than traditional demographic characteristics. Because content threads cross niches, I find that a single article is received differently based on readers' needs and perspectives. They get what they need to get out of it. The same article may be viewed as a marketing article by one reader, while another may view it as a financial article—it's the same article, but each prospect filters the content differently.

Over and over I've had the experience of one person saying: "I read that article and that was my company. We are going through such-and-such." The same person can be talking to someone else, share the article, and the other person says, "No, wait a minute, that's us and it's because of this." Everyone filters all the information you are giving through their individual needs and their wants.

So you reach many more people than expected with an article written from your voice, experience, and expertise. You give them the information; they connect, and it means something to them. As one of my colleagues says, "If they have Velcro on their brain, and it's important to them, it sticks!" Each time something sticks, you have established a relationship with them, because you have given them something they recognize they want to own and they want to do something with.

Wright

How does education marketing make a connection with your market and differentiate you and your business from your competition?

Strickland

The first thing it does is start clarifying in your prospect's mind exactly who you are and defining what it is you can do. They have an ability to read it and say "yes, this applies to me" or it doesn't. The more articles and other content (presentations, handouts, talks, white papers) you get in your prospects' hands, the more opportunities there are to connect. One article may not do it. Multiple articles make a continuous connection. In some instances my markets will see my articles on a daily basis. Others will make contact on a monthly basis through subscriptions to my newsletters. The key is repetition to make and reinforce the connection.

My expertise is business. That isn't general, it is specific. My market gets that through repetition of content—education marketing. People hear me speak on finance, marketing, and other issues. They read articles and newsletters on various business issues. Content brings them in to build their business. It is expertise they can understand and use. Repetition makes an on-going connection. They gain an understanding of what they need and how I can help them. And that's important, because they don't really care why I do it or what my motivation is—they care about what is in it for them. It has to make sense for them. Education marketing, repetition of content really concentrates in their mind that you have what they need. They can read a book, they can come to a workshop, or they can come to an event and get something out of it.

You give away key basic information to get them started. They come back to you to buy your expertise and time. Getting your prospects started demonstrates that you want them to succeed. You care and you understand. And that makes another level of connection, because it's about them—it's not about what I'm selling.

Wright

Let's talk about each of these steps. How do you establish the objectives you wanted to achieve?

Strickland

The first step is to understand your own capabilities and resources. From that foundation you build your credibility and capacity to deliver what the market needs where it is needed. Your market has to want the specific service or solution you are providing. So it's a matter of understanding what your organization wants to be and is capable of delivering—packaging it, connecting with the market, and looking for those opportunities.

Second is to understand the opportunities. Opportunities come from the marketplace and what the competition is and isn't doing. What do and what don't they offer? What is missing that you have the capability and credibility to deliver?

I'm in the consulting field. What I find is that if I look in an ad or look at things other consultants are doing, it pretty much seems they are all interchangeable. That puts you in a commodities market where prices are dictated by your competition. Personally I didn't want to do it that way—I wanted to be out there for my expertise and I wanted to be different. So what I learned was to access what the market was not getting. That is what every business needs to do—fill the niche no one else is filling, penetrate that, and provide something they might not even know they were missing.

Again, this goes back to educating your market. When you educate your market, they start looking around and saying, "Hey, I'm not getting this from anyone else. It might cost a little more, it might take a little more time, it might do this or it might do that, but it's worth it because this is what I need. I don't need this commodity product, I don't need this interchangeable stuff of consultants or services or products (or whatever it is that is out there), I need something that is specific to my needs and is going to help me build my business." That's really what they are looking for, so you start there—you start with knowing what you are capable of delivering and what the market needs.

If the market needs something you are not capable of delivering, then you work on developing those capabilities or acquiring those capabilities. You develop a strategy around packaging that, presenting it, and educating your market.

Again, use all the tools available—and there are so many tools and opportunities available. You key to a strategy that fits your organization and your market. Then you start playing with the tactics to put it out there, to get them to buy, to change things out. You want them to see it. You want to make it through the various filters and perspectives they already have.

Wright

So you recognize not only a market need, but one that prospects, clients, competitors, and the market may not know exists. Where do you go from there?

Strickland

That's the market which has the most opportunity. I say you actually make your own competition when you can recognize an area that is not being served. When you enter that area and begin to have successes, you create an awareness, and again, through education, you are able to build a gradual "Ah ha!" in the market. Prospects say, "Wait a minute, I've not heard this before," or "I've not seen that perspective." Through education, by informing them, the prospects come to you. Again, you provide information and make a connection, and then usually a gradual awareness is built overtime using a series of articles, books, talks, and other materials. You make the information available during speaking engagements, on your Web site, and through publications until something really clicks and they say, "I have to pick up the phone—I have to buy—I need this tool."

I teach my clients to do this with their business. Many have been competing head-on based on price; they are viewed as a commodity business. When they add education marketing to the mix, they start seeing the impact. They recognize the difference it makes when people know they are there for them as their customer. It's not about what the business wants to do and what the business means. It is about the customer, and the business grows as a result of that.

Wright

I remember that there was a speaker many, many years ago who used to say, "Find a need and fill it." Is that what you are talking about?

Strickland

It's that, and finding the need the market doesn't even know exists. They are so accustomed to offerings already in the market, to things not working, defacto products, to products that don't live up to the promise—whether it's a car, or it's a product selling off the shelf in the supermarket—things don't live up to expectations, they really don't change what is going on with that consumer's life or that business's life. If you can find that niche and get them aware that their needs haven't been met, then they are a very powerful group of buyers for your product or your service.

Wright

Will you expand on the "education marketing" concept?

Strickland

I'd be glad to do that. Education marketing means providing information someone needs. It's not about providing information in the format of advertising—it's truly about positioning the information the customers need and demonstrating you know what you are doing and you have the necessary expertise. It's about giving them ideas about what they are doing and what they need to change, whether it's an individual, an institution, the government, or a business—it's making them realize things that could be different and how they can pursue the difference.

It's also about giving your market resources. When you go to my Web site, you will understand why people talk about how much content there is. There are hundreds of articles available at no cost. There is information on workshops, there's information on a variety of topics, there's different things that they can get, and it's all free. They can go there to get information and they can get a feel for things. Each company or each individual can find topics of interest. They can read and take away new information or a different perspective. Again, that makes a connection. We're making available information which normally is not free, somewhere between 10 and 25 percent of the information we have to share. It's basic information—basic things which lay the foundation for what we really want to sell. This enables the client to be more informed, to be more prepared, and to be happier with the service, because they are more aware when they come in and they buy from you.

So you educate them. It's about a process, it's about the product, it's about pitfalls and what to look for, how to evaluate the competition, what to do and what not to do, and what they need to expect. It's about teaching prospects and clients to hold the people they're buying from accountable for their promises. They get to know you, they get to know your expertise, they get to know your ethical standards, and they get to know what you really stand for. All this makes them so much more comfortable. You learn what's going on in their organization, newsletters, press releases, the articles you can run, and information on your Web site. All of those tools together, which are sort of a shotgun approach, have a consistent message which you bear which they need to hear. You provide information that helps them figure out what they need to ask for and what they need to look for.

Wright

How do you get your educational marketing offerings in the hands of prospects?

Strickland

Call, e-mail, and visit the Web site for publication guidelines and editorial calendars. We are fortunate that we are in an age where there are of lots of options. The market is content-hungry on the Internet and in the "traditional" media, there are all sorts of opportunities to publish books and articles—to speak and provide expert opinions. Get your content out there through traditional media, through print media, through radio, through television, through articles, by connecting with them directly about their needs! Contact them to find out how you can help them.

You make the connections and look at those outlets as your customers do. They have needs, and you look to see where they are having the challenges. The media is growing, the Internet appetite for content, the advisory sites, the online magazines—all of these people have a need for content. Make them your customer, make the connection. You can have an article running on hundreds of sites, you can have people request to run it in their newsletters and connect you with their client base.

Opportunities abound, you just have to learn where to look, understand what you are capable of delivering, and make yourself available to those outlets.

Wright

Where do you start making the connections to launch your educational marketing campaign?

Strickland

After the first national article, I concentrated on the local/regional publications. This is especially important if you are going to be focused in a local market. Look for the traditional print publications and the online markets. Identify the publications that are consistent with your markets. Understand the type of content they look for, how frequently they publish, who their audience is. This information may be found on editorial calendars on the Web site or you can request the information. What kind of topics are they looking for? Look at the editorial calendars, look at the local online publications, and see what it is they need. Who are they marketing to?

The next step is to identify how the topics on which I was an expert matched the publication needs. Then make contact: pick up the phone, send an e-mail, submit an article, and follow the processes that of each publication.

You have to understand what market you are going after and who you want to reach. Will it be television, radio, or magazines which will connect you with the market you are trying to pursue? Everyone is looking for content, so when you contact them be prepared with content! Be prepared to tell them: "This is what I can do for you, let me send you this article. Let me send you some substance, some background information on these topics." You are trying to provide information for your customer; let me help you do that.

Wright

Are you saying that the media becomes a customer?

Strickland

They are definitely a customer, and they are a fabulous part of your educational marketing offering, because on a daily basis there are news reports, there are television interviews in local and national markets. The media need experts to go on their shows and talk about current topics. If you can put yourself out there and say, "If you need to call me at three o'clock in the morning to do the morning news show because of a breaking news story, here's my number" then they know you're there. They are going to be calling at three o'clock. But you'd better be there to answer the phone and keep your promise.

The media is another content customer within your market. Same content, different use. You market to the media. You have to build the same credibility with the media as with your other customers. You need to be there and be reliable. Most the time you are doing this without charge, but what you are getting in return is the market exposure, the positioning as an expert, and the opportunity for them to do more stories with you. Then you will be quoted in the print news—to get your name and your expertise out there to people whom you probably would not have been able to reach or afford to reach if you had to buy a slot on the television station to advertise. Media exposure takes you to a higher level of visibility and status. Another bullet, a big bullet, aimed at that target.

An ad on the television station may make someone aware of your business, but that person won't know why he or she needs to buy from you. On the other hand, speaking on a television show or doing a radio show or writing a quick blog for a television news program or online news positions you to provide content and be the expert. It gets you to connect with the audience and gives them information, and gets them comfortable that they know you. The media loves that, they need that. They need qualified, competent, content-driven experts who are available to help them present information to their market and their customers. They become a very enthusiastic supporter of your business, your efforts, and your speaking activities—whatever it is that you are marketing.

Wright

Beyond the traditional print, radio, or television, the Internet provides a platform for effective educational marketing. How do you achieve maximum return on investment when there are so many different communication channels?

Strickland

Two things, be prepared to say "no" to an opportunity that doesn't fit your expertise. Second, keep a consistent message and platform so that when they see you they think "business" or they think "environmental expert" or they think "medical expert"—whatever your expertise is. Make sure that wherever you appear, you understand who the audience is. Who are you are talking to at any point in time? The audience may change depending upon your venue, your message and your positioning must be consistent across all outlets.

With every opportunity you have opportunities to reach beyond your target market. You can write an article for the local paper or for a regional, online news outlet, but it gets read around the world! Everyone's out there searching the internet for information, and one article can lead to speaking engagements, syndication onto other Web sites, and more! There are all kinds of things that one article, one television appearance, or one little blurb quoting you in a news story can do for you—you don't know where it can lead.

You have to be consistent. You have to be on-message, on point, and be willing to say "no" when something isn't your focus. You can't do all things and be all things to all people; you look for synergies across the communications channels. If you can do an interview and turn it into a CD or a tape, it's there for when you are doing a speaking engagement. If you can do an article and use it as marketing material when you are doing a speaking engagement, all these types of things make a consistent image, a consistent approach, a consistent message which really magnifies what you are doing. Every layer emphasizes every other layer. Then they build and spread out, creating a domino effect out into the markets. You just really don't know when you are writing for the local news who may be sitting on the other side of the world Googling for that particular topic and needing something. The interviews you do in national U.S. magazines are read in Asian countries—in India, in Singapore—people are hungry for content. We are fortunate to be in a country where our content gets proliferated out to the various markets and makes it important.

Wright

What does education marketing deliver?

Strickland

The first thing it delivers is visibility. If your name, your face, your company, your message, your content is out there, consistently, then you become "known." Education marketing gets you out there; it gets you ahead of the game because people feel they experience a connection based on what is in it for them. Second, education marketing gives you credibility as an expert in your field. The more people who see you, read your work, see your quotes, the higher your "expert quotient" rises. When they are looking for a speaker, consultant, or resource, your name is going to come right to the top of their mind and they "know" you, so they call.

Third, education marketing improves your success rate in closing deals and improves profits. The prospects who understand what you do and what you can do for them will be the ones who are calling you. Because they know what you do before they contact you, you are going to close at a higher rate and at a better price. Your customer base is more educated and less confused because they have more of an understanding of what needs to happen. You have already provided them with all this information to build on. So the relationship is much more advanced and established because they have that connection.

Fourth comes one of the most unexpected results—when you are doing education marketing, companies and individuals you would have viewed traditionally as competition often become great referrals and allies or execution partners because they are looking to you for your expertise to complement what they do. It magnifies again the marketing channels because you have other companies out there marketing you, because they know they don't do what you do—but their customers need it. So education marketing converts competitors to alliances. Your expertise makes the connection to other experts. Your "competition" now have a resource—you!

Overall, education marketing builds an image, a brand, and a differentiation between all those other things that are out there. Prospects they feel they know you, they've heard your words and they've seen your face, and there's that connection—it's not a cold-call, it's not a mystery relationship. They'll walk up to you and feel they know you because they've read your materials.

Education marketing enables you to charge more for your services/product as you build that image, branding and positioning. You're no longer a commodity, you have marketing power, and you have momentum. People are willing to pay a premium price to bring in someone who is an expert, who is going to make a real difference in their organization. They are more comfortable paying a higher price for a person whom they recognize as an expert, someone who knows what he or she is doing. And that makes a tremendous difference in your business.

Wright

Well, what a great conversation. I always learn when I talk to you. Today we have been talking with Lea Strickland. She is an author, a columnist, and a consultant. She's also president, founder, and CEO of F.O.C.U.S. Resources, a national strategic business consulting practice.

Today we've been talking about marketing strategies and more specifically education marketing. What a great concept! I'm going to think a lot about this, and I may have to call you back and get some more examples.

Strickland

It will be my pleasure.

Wright

Lea, I've really appreciated it and thank you so much for being with us today on Marketing Strategies.

About the Author

LEA STRICKLAND is the founder and President/CEO of F.O.C.U.S.™ Resource, Inc. a national business consulting firm focused on strategic financial and operational issues. Headquartered in the Research Triangle Park region of North Carolina, Lea's clients include for-profit (service and manufacturing) companies, traditional and emerging/growth industries (technology, life science, bio-tech, info-tech, pharmaceutical), not-for-profit, and institutional/government organizations. Lea is a keynote speaker, columnist (over 300 published articles), and author (Out of the Cubicle and Into Business). Lea's practical approach and advice garnered appearances in three issues of Entrepreneur™ in 2005 and 2006 addressing start-up, growth, and management topics. She currently publishes three complimentary newsletters on business issues.

Lea A. Strickland, MBA CMA CFM CBM
F.O.C.U.S. Resources
Cary, North Carolina 27513-4201
Phone: 919.234.3960
E-mail: Lea@FOCUSResourcesInc.com
www.FOCUSResourcesInc.com

Chapter 2

Jay Conrad Levinson

David E. Wright (Wright)

It is a privilege and pleasure to welcome Mr. Jay Conrad Levinson to our program. Jay is the author of the best selling marketing series in history, *Guerrilla Marketing*, plus 24 other business books. His guerrilla concepts have influenced marketing so much that today his books appear in 37 languages and are required reading in many MBA programs worldwide. Jay writes a monthly column for *Entrepreneur Magazine*, articles for *Inc Magazine*, a syndicated column for newspapers and magazines and online columns published monthly on the Microsoft and GTE websites. Recently, Jay has turned much of his attention to the development of the Guerrilla Marketing Association, a dynamic, interactive forum allowing aspiring marketers to learn the fine points of guerrilla marketing directly from Jay from certified coaches, through telephone training sessions, and online publications. And this is just scratching the surface. Jay, I want to thank you for taking the time to speak with us today.

Jay Conrad Levinson (Levinson)

Well, David, thank you for inviting me. I consider it an honor to be engaged in conversation with you.

Wright

Well, thank you. It's unlikely that any of our readers would not be familiar with your ground breaking book, *Guerrilla Marketing*, or one of the other many companion books that you've written sense, but just in case, would you mind telling us a little bit about your background and how you came to write *Guerrilla Marketing?*

Levinson

I'll be happy to. The reality starts on a February day, like today, in Chicago, and the temperature is 13 below zero. I was waiting for a bus, and I had a big job in a giant, wonderful advertising agency in Chicago. Everything was going well, but 13 below zero and the way my ears felt certainly didn't feel like it was going well. So I asked my advertising agency if they would transfer me to San Francisco. They said they couldn't do it because I was too connected with my clients and they didn't want to let me go. So when I said I'd leave and move to San Francisco anyhow, I had accepted a job offer from another advertising agency, the client said, "Hey, Jay, we don't care where you live as long as you continue to write for us." So those were Quaker Oats and Alberto-Culver of Alberto VO5. So I said, "Yes" to them and I decided just to be a consultant to the job that I had accepted. And I found as I started working from my home, which overlooks San Francisco Bay, I'm a hard worker and a fast typist, David. I found that when I was protected from meetings, committees, memos and really nice people coming into my office to shoot the breeze, I could accomplish in three days what used to take me five days. I spent about a year and a half working from my home three days a week, and I thought, "There's nothing really special about me. Everybody ought to try something like this." So I wrote a book about it, *Secret's of Successful Freelancing*, and that book became very successful, but how many freelancers are there? So I expanded the idea in that book and I called it *Earning Money Without a Job*. People said, "Are you the guy who wrote the book Earning *Money without Working?* I said, "Oh no, no! You've got to really work hard, but you don't need a standard nine to five job."

That led to me being invited to teach a course at the University of California in Berkley in their extension division based on *Earning Money Without a Job*. The title of the course was *Alternatives to the 9 to 5 Job*. Then one day my students asked me what sounded like an easy question. It turned out it was not an easy question. They said, "Jay, can you recommend some books for us on marketing a business for people who don't have much money?" And I gave the wrong answer. I said, "Sure." I said, "I'll scout out some books and I'll have them to you the next time we meet." So I went to the library in Berkley, but now we're talking about the early '80s. There were no books on marketing for people with limited budgets. I went to the library at Stanford. I went to the City of San Francisco and Sacramento. I looked in the public libraries. All the books on marketing were written for companies with $300,000 a month to invest. That certainly was not the kids in my classes. So I put together a list of things they might be able to do based on what I had learned working for big companies. At any rate, my list was about 520 ways to market your business that cost very little. Well, that's no title for a book. One day I was reading the newspaper and a man named Blair Newman, who happened to be a boyhood friend of Bill Gates, was quoted as saying that what this economy needs is some kind of guerrilla marketing. And I thought, "Wow! That's a good title for the book." The book I had written for my students was about going after the conventional goals, but using unconventional means. So that became the title of the book for my students.

The book took on a life of its own as my agent found out about it. And gosh! Now it's written in 39 languages, which means I don't understand 38 additions of my own book. But the book was written to satisfy a need. There was a big need of small businesses coming of age in the world. There was a need for inexpensive marketing ideas, and here I was with a book I'd written for most of my students, which fills the world's bill as well.

Wright

Before we get into the nuts and bolts, I would really appreciate hearing your thoughts on the definition of marketing. You know many business people toss around the words "marketing," "sales," "PR," etc., without really understanding the subtle differences between them. In the most practical terms possible, what is your definition of marketing in general, and then what is guerrilla marketing?

Levinson

Well, marketing, David, is any contact that anybody in your business has with anybody else on planet earth. It's not necessarily formalized. It is any contact, how the telephone is answered, the attire worn by your representatives, it's every contact. It's a process. It's not an event. It's not a thing you do a few times a year. It's a continuing, never-ending process. And if you do it right, it's a circle. The circle begins with your ID up for hire to bring income into your life and it becomes a circle when you have the blessed patronage of repeat and referral customers. If you transformed that idea into a circle, you will then understand what marketing is about. So that's what marketing is. It includes a lot of things.

I'll give you the differences between guerrilla marketing and traditional marketing. I used to compare guerrilla marketing with textbook marketing, but I can't do that any more because guerrilla marketing is the textbook in so many university MBA programs. So I have to compare it to traditional marketing. There are 20 differences. These 20 differences, all of them, are just common sense, but these are the real differences. If people can understand these differences and change their business around to do these things, they'll find that their business becomes a whole lot more profitable. In addition, they get a lot more balance in their life because guerrilla marketing is very against the notion of workaholism and being away from your family. It's definitely possible to get work done in standard working hours or less. What marketing preaches strongly is the idea of balance. When I say I've worked a three day week from my home at the edge of a forest overlooking a beautiful blue bay, and I've done it since 1971, I still have to let you know there's nothing really special about me, so thinking anybody ...nobody has to be a workaholic. People who are workaholics choose to do work over everything else in their lives, and I feel sorry because there are lots of other things other than business, other than profits, other than marketing.

Here are the 20 differences between traditional and guerrilla marketing. Number one: Traditional marketing says, "To market you must invest money." Guerrilla marketing says, "Well, if you want to you can, but you don't really have to." Your primary investments should be time, energy, imagination, and knowledge. If you are willing to invest those, you won't have to invest as much if any money.

The second difference: Traditional marketing intimidates a lot of people. As you noticed, David, they're not really sure what it is. It's smoky and it's enshrouded by a mystique. Is sales part of marketing? Is internet presence part of marketing? Well, that mystique disappears with guerrilla marketing because the second difference is that guerrilla marketing completely removes the mystique from marketing. Anybody who's read any guerrilla marketing books or joined the Guerrilla Marketing Association, there's no mystery to marketing for them anymore. They see clearly what it is and what it isn't.

The third difference: Traditional marketing has always been geared to big business, as I mentioned to you when I wrote this book and I was looking for books, I couldn't find any of that were written for people with small budgets. So traditional marketing is geared to big business. Guerrilla marketing is geared very much to small business. Now, although it's true that Fortune 500 Companies buy up several thousand copies of the *Guerrilla Marketing Book* at a time to distribute to their sales and marketing people, the soul and the spirit of guerrilla marketing is in small business. The essence of guerrilla marketing is small business. Now, it's true, a lot of big businesses can use techniques that I'd recommend for small business that cost nothing. They can do that too. Just because they're big companies doesn't mean they have to be a big spender.

The fourth difference: Traditional marketing bases its measurements on sales. Did our sales go down? Or on responses to their offer. How many responses have we got to our offer? Those are on store traffic. How many people came into the store or visited our website? Guerrilla marketing says those are the wrong numbers to look at. There's only one number that tells you the truth, and that is your profits. That bottom line tells us the truth very clearly. A lot of people can enjoy high sales while losing money all along. They can get a lot of responses to an offer, but they may be in a money losing spiral down. So you've got to look at profits because that's the number that lets you know if you're doing it right or you're not doing it right.

The fifth difference: Traditional marketing is based on judgment and experience. That's a fancy way of saying guesswork, and guerrillas can't afford to make wrong guesses. So guerrilla marketing is based as much as possible upon laws of human behavior. Example: we know that 90% of all purchase decisions are made in the unconscious mind. We also know a slam-dunk manner to access the human unconscious mind and the way we do that is through repetition. Now put those two facts together. Decisions are made in the unconscious mind and you can access that unconscious mind through repetition. Then you begin to have a glimmer of an understanding of how the process of marketing works, and that's just one of many examples of how guerrilla marketers use psychology.

A sixth difference: Traditional business has always said, "Grow your business and then diversify." Guerrilla marketing says, "Oh boy! That gets you in over your head and gets you in a lot of trouble." At least the companies like Coca Cola say, "Our name means beverages," and then buying a winery and losing $87 million, and saying, "Well, maybe our name means soft drinks." Other companies have corporate egos that make them think that they can diversify when in reality they are really misdirected if they diversify because the guerrilla answer is forget diversifying. Think about maintaining your focus. Think who you brought to the party and stay with that person. Stay with that focus. It got you to where you are, and your job now is to keep getting better at what you are doing rather than diversifying.

The seventh difference: Traditional marketing has always said the way to grow your business is linearly, which is by adding new customers one at a time. You know, it's the old way. Well, that's a pretty expensive way to grow. Guerrilla marketers know there are better ways to grow a business. They grow their businesses geometrically. That means they enlarge the size of each transaction. They aim to have more transactions per sales cycle with their customers, and they tap the enormous referral power of each one of those customers. Each one is the center of a network, and they grow linearly in the old fashioned way. Now they are growing in four directions at once: larger transactions, more transactions, referral transactions, and standard linear transactions. It's pretty impossible to lose money, let alone go out of business if you understand just that idea about growing geometrically.

The eighth difference: Traditional marketing believes marketing is over once they have made the sale. Because of that mindset, 68% of business that is lost in the United States is lost not due to poor service and not due to shabby quality. It's lost due to customers being ignored after they've made the purchase. That's why guerrilla marketing preaches fervent follow up so you can get in touch with those customers and let them know you appreciate their business. Life is not just all business. Connect up with them as a human being as well. Follow up and let them know that you really care and that you're grateful, and you're not going to lose 68% of your business like so many other businesses do. It's just the human thing to do.

Wright

We're kind of privileged to visit with you today, Jay, because many of our readers and clients have tremendous products to sell to people. These are people who have invested years of their lives and a great deal of their own money getting the product ready, but then they hit the wall which is marketing, and they are rarely prepared. Have you found this to be true? What would you tell someone who has run into this wall?

Levinson

I'd say it's a really easy wall to surmount because all it takes is a simple plan, not a complex plan. Guerrillas start with a very simple seven step marketing plan. That's all. Once you start with the plan, then you've got to promise yourself that you will commit to that plan because that's what really makes marketing work. That's what really makes marriage work. That's what really makes a business work, or completing a marathon. It's a commitment to your plan. You must be committed and that's how you get over the wall. The plan is your stepladder over it and the commitment to the plan is how you get down the other side and make it to the finish line. But there is no finish line because guerrilla marketers know that the journey is the goal. People do run into a wall in marketing, and you know, David, you can't blame them for seeing that wall because they think marketing is complicated. But as I was showing, we just talked about eight of the ways guerrilla marketing is different from traditional marketing. The point still being that if you break it down into simple components, what guerrilla marketing does starting with a seven steps marketing plan, then that wall isn't as high. It's more easily surmountable. You have a road map. You know where to go. Gosh without a plan, that's like taking a journey without having a road map. It's not going to work out.

Wright

So does guerrilla marketing explain the seven steps?

Levinson

Oh, yes. It tells you just the seven different steps. Seven simple sentences that you've got to complete. All of them are short sentences except for the fourth sentence, and once you've finished those sentences, are you ready for this? It takes five minutes to write a guerrilla marketing plan. I've taught this at Berkley for ten years and I gave these students five to write a seven sentence guerrilla marketing plan. They all did it and many of them used that same seven sentence marketing plan for the next many years in guiding their business because it gave them a map into uncharted terrain. I know you've discovered that doing business is pretty much uncharted terrain. There are lots of surprises out there and they say it's a jungle out there. That's why guerrilla warfare is necessary to proceed faithfully in that jungle towards your goal. I wrote *Guerrilla Marketing* to make it as simple and safe as possible. I'm telling you one of the big things that as you launch a guerrilla marketing attack to do it with slow motion. Don't be in a hurry. My average client takes a year and a half to launch a really successful guerrilla marketing attack, and my newest book, *Guerrilla Marketing for Free*, talks about a hundred ways you can market for zero, zero cost. It's not as complicated as they think. And it's getting easier now than ever before for a small business to really make inroads into a big world and get a small chunk of a very large pie, or if they want a large chunk. But don't forget, I think the most important thing is to necessarily just to build your business and increase your profits, but also to have that balance in your life.

Wright

So, what I hear you saying is that you believe the reason most people don't take it upon themselves to learn how to be successful marketers is they think it's too … it's overly technical or complicated or too time consuming?

Levinson

Yes. Yes, that's exactly right, David.

Wright

I scanned amazon.com before calling you today, and I was amazed at how many guerrilla titles you've produced. Would you mind picking one or two of these titles and telling our readers how you translated the basic guerrilla philosophy into other marketing applications like internet marketing, home based business marketing? In other words, can your strategies really work across the business models?

Levinson

Yes, they really can because of the reason they were written. As I told you, I wrote the first guerrilla marketing book in 1984, but those books have sold 16 million copies so far. I wrote the first one to satisfy me, which happened to be a need in my classroom, just to learn about marketing inexpensively. Later I started giving talks because as an instructor at Berkley you get invitations to give talks at conventions that are passing through the San Francisco Bay area. I would give talks and people would ask me to be more specific about the weapons of guerrilla marketing. They said, "You sure talk about a lot of the weapons. I wonder if you could describe them." So I wrote another book called, *Guerrilla Marketing Attack*, which describes the weapons of guerrilla marketing, and the myths as you and I are talking about, and some of the psychology that I brought up. Then the feedback I got, people said, "Boy, that's great when you talk about the weapons. Would you consider doing a chapter on each weapon?" I like writing sensationally. So I wrote 100 chapters – there's 100 weapons – but only of maybe two and a half pages each. There's a description of each weapon that a business might need.

And then I noticed that a lot of people were reading the books, taking it seriously, growing their business, and they were ready to just move up to the next level. So I thought, "Wow! A lot of these people know how to do it now, so I'm going to show them how to do it with excellence." So I wrote a book about the golden rules of marketing called, *The Guerrilla Marketing Excellence, the 50 Golden Rules of Guerrilla Marketing*. Then, as you identified, suddenly here comes the internet and nobody has a clue how to really do it right. It's just a sure path to financial oblivion if you do it wrong. So my publisher said, "Can you do a book to help people do it right?" So I knew I could, but I know how long it would take for me to learn it. But I knew a person also who had been teaching, also who had several books on computers. He'd been on the internet since the '80s, and his name was Charlie Ruben. I said, "Charlie, would you help me do a book about guerrilla marketing online?" And he said, "I'd love to." And together we did *Guerrilla Marketing Online* and *Guerrilla Marketing Online, Second Edition* and *Guerrilla Marketing Online Weapons*. And along comes my friend, Seth Godin. Seth Godin said, "Yeah." He said, "There's so many home based businesses and they can use a lot of the techniques you write about. Let's collaborate on a book for home based businesses." So we wrote *Guerrilla Marketing for Home Based Businesses*. And Orville Ray Wilson from Colorado, who's a master salesperson and believes in the guerrilla techniques wants to collaborate with another author, Bill Gallagher, on guerrilla selling because so many people sell, and they need a lot of these guerrilla characteristics in their selling to literally double their sales output with new ideas. And so we wrote *Guerrilla Selling*. That's been a very successful book.

These books are written to fill a void, and in response to what people need. Technology has undergone a revolution in the past 10 years, not because it's become more powerful or pretty or graphical. It's because it's become less complicated. So I wrote a book about that. I didn't come through with any background of technology. I had a totally different kind of background, but I wrote a book for people like me who had no technical background. I called it, *Guerrilla Marketing with Technology,* because I felt that there was a need for such a book. The one I just talked about, *Guerrilla Marketing for Free,* was because I know some people really want to start out with a shoestring and they're wearing loafers, so they have no shoestring. So they can't spend anything except what I said: time, energy, imagination, and knowledge.

Last week a new book that I wrote came out that I co-authored with two people called, *Guerrilla Retailing*, because retail businesses across America are being hit hard and most of them just are in the dark as to how to compete against the Wal-Marts, the big box stores, and they need help. And so we came riding up on our white horse and hopefully provided *Guerrilla Retailing*. So those titles are in response to needs and that's the key to all business, David. If you can find the needs, then go into business just filling them. Don't try to create your product or your business and then look around for people who want them. It's much easier first to find the need, then to create your product or your service.

Wright

Let's talk a little bit about the Guerrilla Marketing Association. When you spoke to the office earlier, you seemed really excited about this resource. How does it come about? What can it mean to an aspiring business person?

Levinson

Well, I love the question because it's the way my life has changed. I've written 31 books. That's about a book a year since I started doing this. I realized that, when I see my book at Barnes & Noble, I see things in the book that maybe three, four, or five things that I wish I hadn't said because those things have changed since then. It takes about a year or a year and a half from the time the book leaves my work word processor to the time it's on the shelves at Borders, Barnes & Noble or Books-a-Million. I also think of about five things that I hadn't put in that book, and the reason I didn't put them in the book is that I didn't know them then.

I feel that I did my best in writing the books, but still I wish I could be more in touch with the readers. The Guerrilla Marketing Association enables me to do that. It's a way for me to write, but have my writings published monthly, and not only write and publish monthly, but to get questions from people who have read and give them answers immediately. Here's what the Guerrilla Marketing Association is. It's a small service for small business, an interactive service where people join as members. As members here's what they get. Once a month they get a publication online. It's called the *Guerrilla Marketing Insider*. At least 30 cutting edge ideas that are on three things. They're *Cutting Edge New*, they're able to be put to use the next day or that day, and they cost either nothing or very little. They get at least 30 of those, plus they get five videos, which they view online, interviews with experts just to make it more interesting and let them really hear it from the horse's mouth some of the home truths about marketing. In addition to that, there's a coaching forum, which means they can ask questions about their business. They can say, "Hey, here's my website. What do you think of it?" They'll usually get an answer within 24 hours. We have a team of 40 coaches, certified coaches, who answer those questions. These are college professors, or authors, or ex Fortune 500 people who love answering marketing questions, and they answer questions for our members on a regular basis. We also have a Wednesday evening phone call. The members on the call can then ask questions of all of us, and they can ask questions specific to their business.

Here's how good this is. Last month we had a member on who said, "Well, I've just written a book and my goal is to get it to be number one at Barnes & Noble. Does anybody have any suggestions?" Well, we happened to have a couple of people on the call as experts, who were in the field of literature and the field of bookselling. And we have some members who had quite a bit of experience in making books grow, who told this member on the phone their ideas for what he might do to boost the sales of his book, especially Barnes & Noble. Two weeks later, the call comes up. He's on the phone. He says, "I want to thank you guys for the help you gave me." He says, "My book is number one best seller at Barnes & Noble." We were amazed, but that was the reality. This is what we're set up to do. We give information that is immediately actionable. We charge $49.97 a month. You can quit whenever you want and there's no long-term contract or anything. Our website has a new idea called the tip of the day. Every single day you go to the website you're going to learn something you didn't know before.

There's also a whole course on guerrilla marketing free for the asking right on the site. It's part of the membership. Our several hours of videos are of a very expensive ($4,000.00) boot camp that I gave in Las Vegas. The video of that is also on there.

Weekly, people get updated on marketing of an e-mail newsletter, we send a very short one once a week. So those are some of the things people get when they join the association. They get access to me. I really am the father of guerrilla marketing, but I'm interacting with them on the phone and on the coaching forum and on the things I write in *The Insider*. So there is a back and forth and we get to be even more responsive to what the members want to learn about, what they want to do, what they need most. And if I don't know the answers, and we both know… neither one of us knows the answers, that's why they have experts and other certified coaches who can answer the ones that I can't answer.

Wright

Before we let you go this afternoon, will you give our readers one last bit of advice? What else would you say to encourage men and women who are serious about trying new ideas to market their goods and services but haven't been able to get off square one?

Levinson

Well, it's a matter of not realizing that it's a big job, but that it's a step by step job. There's ten steps to take to succeed with a guerrilla marketing attack, and it shouldn't take you a long time to do it. Every part of this is easy, except for the eighth step. If you take these steps, one by one by one by one, you'll find that marketing is easy and that you are able to make it work for you.

The first step is to research your market, your product, research the competition, research your prospect and the website of their competitors, research your own benefits.

Step two is to write a benefits list, which is a list of the benefits people gain by doing business with you. And then put a circle around all those benefits that are also competitive advantages, advantages not offered by your competition.

Now, the third step is to select the weapons that you are going to use. I told you, you can find a list of 100 of them at the guerrillamarketingassociation.com. Select the ones you'll use and then put them in priority order, just put a date next to each one of them so you'll know when you're going to launch it.

The fourth is where you create that seven sentence guerrilla marketing plan. That's pretty darn simple. Seven sentences. First sentence tells the purpose of your marketing. The second tells the benefits or competitive advantages. You'll stress to achieve your purposes. The third sentence tells your target audience. Fourth sentence tells your marketing weapons you'll use. The fifth sentence tells you your niche in the marketplace, what you stand for. The sixth sentence tells you your identity, not your image. That's a phony thing. I said your identity, truth and honesty, who you really are. You have a personality. You've just got to be aware that you have one and you're in charge of what it is. Communicate that in your identity. The seventh sentence tells your marketing budget, and it should be expressed as a percent of your projected gross sales. In 2003, the average American business invested 4% of their gross sales in marketing. 4%. So think of how much you'll invest in 2004. Okay, now you've done a marketing plan which is the fourth step.

The fifth step is make a guerrilla marketing calendar. There's an easy way for you to make one and print it out for yourself at the Guerrilla Marketing Association website that lets you plan out ahead a year for what you're going to be doing. It makes everything easy so you don't have to make a lot of decisions.

The sixth step is finding fusion-marketing partners, people who have the same kind of prospect as you or same kind of standards as you, and go into joint marketing arrangements with them. There's a lot of that going on in America today, especially the area of small business. What is does it lets more people know your work and it reduces the cost because you're sharing it with other people.

The seventh step is now to launch your marketing attack in slow motion. You've got to feel comfortable about it emotionally that you're not doing too much, and you've got to feel comfortable about it financially that you're not spending too much. And you won't if you understand guerrilla marketing.

Here comes the hard part. I warned you the eighth step is the real tough one. It stops most people. Talk about a wall. It's maintain your attack. Most people expect marketing to work instantly, and it doesn't work instantly so they quit what they did even though everything they did was right. It takes a lot, but you've got to be committed to it. You've got to maintain the attack. More money is lost in this area than any other area. This is where it stops. Doing everything that's right and seeing that nothing has happened.

Okay, the ninth step, now this is hard, keep track because you're going to use a whole lot of weapons. You're going to hit the bull's eye with some of them and you're going to miss the target with others. Unless you keep track, you're not going to know which is which. So you must know the bull's eyes for the misses because guerrilla marketing is not a matter of using a lot of marketing weapons. It's a matter of being aware of a lot, trying many, and then getting rid of the ones that didn't hit the center of the bull. And keeping track is the name of the game.

Now you get to the tenth step. The tenth step is now that you've done all of these things I just mentioned, start improving in all areas. Improve your message. Improve the media you are using, which means using fewer. This way you can improve your budget. You can spend less and you improve your results. You get more. Real successful companies don't invest a lot of money in marketing. They went through this process I just told you about, a ten step one by one process.

They weren't in a hurry, and then they found out that boy marketing is easier than I thought it was. It's the best investment available in America today if you do it right and you just heard how to do it right.

Wright

Boy, I'll tell you. That's a doctorate in marketing. We've been talking today with Mr. Jay Conrad Levinson. It's been an absolute delight, Jay. I really appreciate it. Thank you so much for sharing your thoughts and insights with us.

Levinson

Well, thank you for giving me the opportunity to talk about my core marketing beliefs, David.

About the Author

JAY CONRAD LEVINSON is the author of the best-selling marketing series in history, "Guerrilla Marketing," plus 24 other business books. His guerrilla concepts have influenced marketing so much that today his books appear in 37 languages and are required reading in many MBA programs worldwide.

Jay taught guerrilla marketing for ten years at the extension division of the University of California in Berkeley. And he was a practitioner of it in the United States—as Senior Vice-President at J. Walter Thompson, and in Europe, as Creative Director at Leo Burnett Advertising.

He writes a monthly column for *Entrepreneur Magazine*, articles for *Inc. Magazine*, a syndicated column for newspapers and magazines and online columns published monthly on the Microsoft and GTE websites.

Jay has served on the Microsoft Small Business Council and the 3Com Small Business Advisory Board. His Guerrilla Marketing is series of books, a videotape, an award-winning CD-ROM, a newsletter, a consulting organization, an Internet website, and a way for you to spend less, get more, and achieve substantial profits.

Here is the man to transform you into a marketing guerrilla—Jay Conrad Levinson.

Jay Conrad Levinson
Guerrilla Marketing International
369-B 3rd Street #301
San Rafael, California 94901
Phone: 415.455.9197
www.guerrillamarketingassociation.com

Chapter 3

Rod Jones

David Wright (Wright)

Today we're talking with Rod Jones, chief learning officer of Mori Seiki University. His passion is to help managers, employees, distributors and customers increase their personal and business performance through value-driven learning.

Mori Seiki U.S.A. is a world leader in high-technology manufacturing systems and Rod's leadership at their corporate university requires developing advanced, blended learning experiences across a broad range of business disciplines. Learning is central to Mori Seiki's value proposition. Prior to joining Mori Seiki, Rod spent 15 years at the helm of Decision Technology a respected industrial sales and marketing consulting firm serving technology-based clients in hyper-competitive markets.

He is a co-author of *Speaking of Success* with Steven Covey and Ken Blanchard.

Rod Jones (Jones)

Thank you David, it's a pleasure to talk with you today.

Wright

We often speak of value when selling our products and services. Is there something we are missing when we talk about value?

Jones

David, "value" is a word that's fundamental to business, but many don't really know what it means. The word has, in a sense, lost its value.

Several years ago I asked the president of a medium-sized manufacturer what value he offered to his customers—his value proposition. He didn't know and instead he told me it was the salesperson's job to answer that question. Evidently, it was the salespeople's gift of gab that was supposed to drum up value into a smooth package and deliver it to customers. This constitutes backward logic. How can a salesperson communicate value to the customer if company management can't create, define, and communicate it?

Overall, businesses suffer from four issues. First, companies fail to define value; second, they can't quantify it; third, they do not align this value to customer needs; and four, they fail to communicate that value effectively.

Wright

What kind of issues contribute to these four problems?

Jones

There are a number of contributing factors. Sometimes companies fail to discover and describe the high value already inherent in their product. Other times, however, attempting to discover and define value brings to the footlights what managers fear most: lack of differentiation. The global market is turning products into commodities faster than ever, and that destroys differentiation. Many find their products are similar to everyone else's, so they sell on price.

Communicating value for low-priced leaders is relatively straightforward. These companies sell "me too" products—their sole value to end-users remains low price. But the lowest-price business also remains one of the most cut-throat, particularly for manufacturers. Today, you may sell the cheapest widget, but tomorrow a competitor may enter the market and offer something cheaper— shattering your product's sole value in one fell swoop.

Some businesses thrive on this, of course, including the world's biggest company, Wal-mart. But market economics only allow room for one or two low-priced leaders. For this reason, all others must strive for value through product differentiation and customer service.

When defining and communicating value, missteps occur. Many people think companies "create" value; the sales and marketing department's job is then to sell that value to customers. But doing so, in fact, goes against the grain of a natural business transaction. In reality, no product or service on earth would have any value if there weren't customers willing to buy them.

In other words, *customers define value, not sellers.*

Wright

Doesn't value simply represent the selling price?

Jones

It's not that simple. At its core, value represents an exchange. Think of a balancing scale, with the customer's hard-earned money on one side and a product or service on the other. When the customer perceives the balance is right, an exchange will take place—not before. The goal should be to discover and communicate product value so that the transaction takes place at the right time and for the right reasons.

During the transaction, it's important to demonstrate a true respect for a customer's hard-earned money, particularly in a business-to-business transaction. Customers build their business with blood, sweat, and tears and they do not, nor should they, spend money easily. If a salesperson just wants an order, it becomes all about the seller—and not the potential customer.

For example, in industrial markets, it's critical for sales and marketing personnel to visit the customer's facility to see the processes and operational challenges and, most importantly, spend time with those who actually make the product. They must build an emotional attachment to it. Potential customers can sense this emotional attachment and, at that moment, begin relating to the salesperson. Once the salesperson relates to a customer's pain and respects their hard-earned money, the customer detects it with a kind of "sixth sense." This is when the customer is ready to hear the value story.

Wright

How prominent are emotions when customers establish value?

Jones

A customer *perceives* value first before digging into the facts. True, quantifiable facts about a product or service do provide the foundation for value; but by themselves they are just that—a flat foundation, not relating to anything and not always very interesting. Above the facts is perception, or how the customer perceives the product.

Think back to the "cola wars." Remember the "Pepsi Challenge"? The company did extensive blind taste tests, showed them in their advertisements, revealing factual research that more consumers favored Pepsi's taste over Coke—but Coke, being the older and more established brand, remained the market leader. Why? The Pepsi Challenge presented consumers with the facts without first addressing perception. True, Pepsi was the sweeter product; it did win the majority of taste tests. But Coke was the first brand to market, Coke was the most recognizable brand on the planet—Coke *was* America. For this reason, customers perceived the product as the original and all others as followers.

A few years later, the tables turned. Pepsi changed its marketing strategy to the "Pepsi Generation" (i.e., young people). That hit the bull's eye of public perception—Pepsi is for young people and, by default, older people because older people often think of themselves as young. Coke hit back, targeting its soft drink on youth, but it was too late. Pepsi created a new category—youth—and Coke was on the defensive. Pepsi's market share gain had nothing to do with the product's actual attributes.

Sometimes, innovative design wins. Consider Dutch Boy paint. Several years ago the company redesigned their product packaging so that instead of a regular paint can, the company used a plastic container with a comfortable handle and no-drip spout, similar to those used for liquid laundry detergent. This feature added tremendous value; it saved the customers' time and made their job easier. Perceived value and, hence, sales increased. The product (paint) inside the container was the same.

A product need not be redesigned to add value. In fact, companies should go for the low-hanging fruit first, one being so-called "hidden" value—value that exists in the product but has just never been discovered and communicated to the customer. One place to look for hidden value is in a product's total cost of ownership. Particularly for large purchases, studies show that over a product life cycle the initial price may only account for 15 to 20 percent of the total cost of ownership.

Why then is selling all about initial purchase price? What about the costs of owning, operating, and maintaining the product? Does the product or its support services help reduce these in any way? Spelling these savings out helps the customer see more of the product's value. The product hasn't changed, but the value to customers will increase dramatically.

Wright

Once we discover value, what's the best way to communicate its power?

Jones

Perhaps more than in the consumer marketplace, marketers—particularly in engineering and technical sectors—fall victim to "feature overload." They speak about specifications and other facts while not paying attention to how customers perceive their product. This happens because the salesperson is ignoring one immutable fact: product specifications serve little purpose when communicating value unless they meet specific customer needs.

At a recent trade show, numerous show-goers asked me how our company could solve their manufacturing problems. I could tell many were expecting me to rattle off a list of details about the features and services we offer—but I didn't. Instead, I asked what their company did, and what manufacturing process challenges gave them the most headaches during the workday. Those questions helped me communicate only those details that would immediately affect those headaches. In other words, I aligned our value to meet *specific* customer needs. Among other things, this makes the oral communication between you as a marketer and the customer more efficient because every point you make solves a particular problem. This is a process called *alignment* and it amplifies value.

According to studies, during a sales presentation, customers perceive a product's value in different ways: about 55 percent of it comes from what the customer sees (visual factors); about 38 percent of it comes from the presenter's tone of voice and inflection, and the remaining 7 percent comes from the words. That means just under a tenth of the brain perceives value through the actual words a salesperson says. That's not much. The bottom line: what a customer sees, visually, remains the primary driver of perceived value.

Wright

How does a company capitalize on the customer's perceived value?

Jones

To illustrate, consider a lawn-cutting and landscaping company. Companies like this distribute flyers with their company name and all the services they provide: mowing, trimming, edging, hedge-clipping and pruning, and so on, and at the bottom it might say something like, "Call for a free estimate" in big letters. The potential customer sees two things: a long list of services and the word "estimate." The long list by itself could imply "expensive." With that, the customer throws the flyer in the trash.

Now, if that same company sends out another flier with a picture of a man relaxing on a lawn chair—again, the all-important visual component—and the words, "Take Back Your Weekend," with the company name and number with a minimal feature list, the picture and text say it all. The company solves a major problem for the customer, so they don't think about price. Instead, the potential customer is more likely to call the number on the flyer, simply because he or she would like to, as the flyer says, take back their weekend. More recreational time is the value driver.

Facts are necessary in marketing to effectively communicate value. But for most people, facts alone will never trigger the emotion needed for them to buy a significant product or service.

Wright

Do these concepts apply to all customers universally?

Jones

Some do, some don't. The nature of this emotion comes out when examining how different buyers behave. In general, they can be grouped into four categories:

First, there are the "innovators," those who want the next new product first (e.g., the people who stood in line to be the first to get a new iPhone). These people thrive on innovation and change—but not necessarily for the long-term.

They may buy on impulse, and being the very first adopters of new products and services, they take higher risks. They thrive on innovation, which triggers an immediate need for ownership that may not be based on realistic needs. This results in overestimating or misinterpreting a product's value, which can result in a poor investment. (Case in point: innovators lost when Apple cut the iPhone price several months after its release.). They may not be the best marketing target because they change their minds quickly and often.

Next are the "early adopters." In the business-to-business world, these people make up the majority of trade show attendees examining the new technology available. If a product can meet their current or future needs, they perceive the product to have high value. They like buying new things and they feel innovative products represent a positive investment. More often than not, they are looked upon as industry leaders, always several steps ahead of the competition. Of all the buyers, these should represent a successful sales-and-marketing campaign's bread and butter. They invest heavily and smartly. They know how to align a product's value with their business-growth strategy. In short, they represent stable, lucrative, long-term business relationships as long as solid and useable product innovation is offered.

The "early majority" make up the next category. These people follow what the early adopters are doing. They invest in new products only after others whom they know to be successful have done the same and they have reasonable evidence to justify their purchase. They perceive a product's value, but "propping" up that perception is the fact that others are using the product and have proved its success.

Within the "late majority" category, skepticism enters the picture. Looking at and buying products and services aren't fun for these people; they do it with pressure from competitors and customers. New technology needs to be heavily proven and justified before they make an investment. If a new product represents a departure from the conventional way of doing things, these people may not invest in it until their early-adopter competitors are already investing in next-generation technology. The bottom line: they perceive product value with a skeptical eye, and laying money on the table doesn't come easy.

The final category, the "laggard," represents those who view new product purchasing as a necessary evil. They buy new technology and products only when forced to. In the business world, these usually represent companies with management that accepts change reluctantly. Their perception of new products always starts in negative territory, and if it ever turns positive, it only does so when they see undeniable proof of that product's value in action. They may buy used products before new.

Identifying which customers fall into which category requires sales and marketing to work together researching, interviewing, and observing customers. When building your marketing strategy, pay attention to how each category perceives value. Does the company or individual have the latest and greatest equipment, or do they use outdated business processes or technology? How do others perceive the company? Code your customer database with the product adoption types and then target your existing or new products to the right customer type.

Wright

What are some practical ways to identify value-driven, early adopter customers?

Jones

Sometimes, the easiest thing to do is simply ask existing customers, "Who is the market leader in your field?" Their answer will give you the "crème de la crème" of your customer base; most will be early adopters. Particularly in the business-to-business sector, these market leaders represent progressive, stable businesses, and if they make up the majority of your customer base, your business will likely experience similar success. Most importantly, they perceive product value and know how to link it to their business.

Conversely, why spend any time and money marketing to a laggard? He or she may buy a used product or only buys new when forced—and in today's market, that's often too late.

When selling business-to-business, perception also changes when talking with different levels of management within an organization. Communicating value to a CEO or upper manager can be quite different than someone in purchasing or operations. It boils down to what each person's "pain points" are, what he or she thinks about on the job, day in and day out. Put another way, each looks for something that will make reaching his or her objectives easier. For those in upper management, they're thinking about return on investment, P&L, cash flow, and business growth. For managers and owners, value should be communicated in those terms. If a product increases cash flow their jobs become easier. This eases a pain point and triggers an emotion that perceives high value in your product. For many operations people, if a product (e.g., automated machinery) simplifies operations on the factory floor and allows that person to do more in less time, the product does indeed make operations people's job more successful. This again spurs emotions and a perception of high product value. Change your message to fit the value perception of each customer level.

Wright
What can go wrong with the value-building process?

Jones
As mentioned earlier, customers perceive value first and then look for facts to support their perception. It is the job of marketing and sales to build value in the customer's mind. At the moment, when the money changes hands or when the product is delivered, a customer's perception of value is at its highest. Customers have heard and bought into your value proposition, and they have viewed the details that back it up. But shortly thereafter, it often drops sharply. Why?

There are two culprits. First, something in the pre-sale process may have misled the customer with incomplete or inaccurate facts. Overselling or over-marketing can be costly. Value drops when customers' expectations don't match what they think they were promised. Second, a bad experience during initial ownership. For instance, a poor installation experience with complex technical equipment. These bad experiences during initial ownership send value into a nosedive.

Some drop in value is, for the most part, unavoidable. Our excitement with a new product tends to wane with time. But through careful research, planning, product design, and communication, a company can minimize that drop drastically.

The most critical point in the customer satisfaction timeline is the installation of a product or the first days of product ownership. If this goes well, loyalty is maintained; if it goes poorly, loyalty may be lost for months or years to come. Brainstorming sessions can work wonders here. Preparation for the session should include customer interviews, focus groups, and other research. These interviews aren't trying to "sell" the product; they are simply trying to find those nagging customer annoyances that make perceived value drop.

Wright

Brainstorming sessions can be difficult to control, so exactly how do you stay focused on discovering value?

Jones

Staying focused is definitely the key. During the brainstorming session, draw a timeline of activities your customer takes to acquire your product: research, sales visits, factory visits (for large capital-purchase items), demonstrations, proposals, approvals, purchasing, training, installation, service calls, payment, and everything in between. (Often the process may involve twenty—yes twenty—or more steps!) Having people from all departments in the room helps judge how many times and in what manner the customer must interact with your company. Include a few good customers in these meetings.

The timeline could uncover a product design feature that could be improved or it could show a cryptic billing statement (nothing is more annoying than a bill that can't be deciphered). What about hard-to-read instructions or inadequate training that prevents customers from using all the features of a product? For instance, what if customers bring a product home and unpack it only to find they need a tool or battery? A small investment to include batteries in the box can make customers much happier, and a happier customer base is sure to make back that small investment many times over.

All these inefficiencies represent losses of value and the team's goal is to improve the buying process, make the entire transaction easier, and to reduce or eliminate value-killers.

Today manufacturers are adopting the principles of lean manufacturing, eliminating waste on the shop floor, and identifying and maximizing "value streams." This lean process in effect extends the value stream to the customer. If not, customers' perception of value for your product isn't likely to change, which in turn makes it difficult for your business to grow.

Here's an important point: these sessions *uncover* the value needed by the customers, which is the only real value. Capitalism is a two-way street between buyer and seller and value requires both. If a product involves incredible, innovative technology, but no one perceives any value in it, the product—including all the work that went into it—is worthless.

Wright

Earlier while discussing emotions, you stated that facts are the foundation for establishing value. How are facts used to build value?

Jones

As mentioned, a high-value product must have "the facts"—features, specifications, etc.—to support it. But the facts by themselves aren't enough. For a truly effective value proposition, value must be quantified, particularly for high-dollar or capital-intensive purchases. And as with any business transaction, that value must translate into dollars and cents.

Initially, people perceive value based on the price tag—the higher the price, the higher value the product must have to trigger a purchase. But what about all the design and process improvements discussed in that brainstorming session and similar improvement efforts? Are they included in the price? How about the dollars saved over a product's life cycle, that "hidden value" within a product's total cost of ownership? Say your product uses less energy than competing brands. Do the math and turn that percentage into real dollars: "Over a ten-year product life cycle, with an average energy cost of 'X,' your total energy savings will be 'Y,' and your total cost-of-ownership savings will be 'Z' dollars."

For large purchases, don't forget about resale value. Think about cars or large machinery—the more resale value the product has, the higher the purchase value. Quantify it by showing the average percentage of depreciation, then the price of the resale after so many years. In business, numbers are real. The more you quantify the better.

In my field—factory automation and computerized machine tools—many sellers provide "value added" services at no charge in order to win an order. Selling manufacturing technologies can become extraordinarily complex. For example, a company may invest thirty hours of engineering time to prove it can solve a customer's problem. This costs the seller, say $3,000, but that amount is never communicated to the customer. If the customer has no idea how much the service would have "normally" cost, he or she will take those expensive giveaway value-added services for granted; in other words, the customer perceives them to have no value. And sometimes, customers will gradually expect more of them until margins for the transactions become seriously squeezed. Instead, forward an "invoice" to the customer showing the price, but note on the invoice that the customer is not being charged. This effectively communicates how much this service costs; in turn, the customer perceives he or she is getting *even more* value.

Wright

Is it possible to spend time and money creating products with high value content, but then fail to get the message to potential customers?

Jones

It happens all the time. Here are a few tips to get customers' attention. Ever wonder why the iPhone gets so much play in the media? What is it about Steve Jobs? Besides having dominating charisma, the man has one asset that media flock to—vision. A positive, gleaming vision of the future overarches everything at Apple nowadays, and it has drawn loyal customers and media people who give plenty of coverage. That vision transcends the product—this isn't just about marketing, it's a representation of better things to come. Apple's products—and Microsoft's and those of other rivals—can be billed as "the future," since, in fact, their products have and probably continue to change many of the ways humans interact, via the Internet, cell phones, PDAs, and other devices.

Not many products can relate to such lofty thinking, but the thinking does illustrate why Apple receives so much media coverage. The company relates the product value to overarching business themes.

Consider a press conference at an industry trade show. Press releases are handed out highlighting product features and then a company executive starts talking, describing those features. For the press, this seldom raises eyebrows and the result might simply be a short product review in a trade journal.

What the media people want and what they value are those overarching themes—the common customer pain points, broad business issues, and, if possible, a vision for the industry. Ultimately, press conferences (and in any communication with media, for that matter) should relate those business themes or vision to the product value with the hope that media will convey those points to their audience. The more powerful the vision, the more media pays attention. The media plays a key role in building up a product's value across a broad customer base.

Wright

Can a business be successful without a solid value proposition?

Jones

David, in today's global market, it would be very difficult. The concept of value makes sales and marketing jobs immensely challenging, but also the most rewarding. A general mistrust of marketing still permeates in many business sectors. Marketing and salespeople are dubbed "spin doctors"—people who twist the numbers and "rephrase" the facts just to close the sale. Some may, but they aren't likely to see long-term success.

Today's true sales and marketing professional sees value for what it is—the keystone of business. Without it, everything around it crumbles, and a company ends up selling on price, entering a "race to the bottom." And as described, the market doesn't have room for too many winners in that race.

Fundamentally, it all boils down to a phrase: sell value, not price. The concept may ultimately require a re-education of your entire company, but the result will unleash a continuous stream of customer value—the ultimate differentiator.

About the Author

ROD JONES, chief learning officer of Mori Seiki University is a unique individual whose successful career spans sales, marketing and education.

Mori Seiki U.S.A. is a world leader in high-technology manufacturing systems and Rod's leadership at their corporate university requires developing advanced, blended learning for employees, distributors and customers. Learning is central to Mori Seiki's value proposition. Prior to joining Mori Seiki, Rod spent 15 years at the helm of Decision Technology a respected industrial sales and marketing consulting firm serving technology-based clients in hyper-competitive markets.

Helping managers, sales professionals and employees increase their personal and business success through learning is his expertise. Rod has consulted and spoken to the Association for Manufacturing Technology, the American Machine Tool Distributors' Association, the Society of Manufacturing Engineers and the University of Michigan. He is a co-author of "Speaking of Success" with Steven Covey and Ken Blanchard.

Rod Jones
Mori Seiki University
5655 Meadowbrook Drive
Rolling Meadows, IL 60008-3833
847.593.5400 Main
847.472.9675 Fax
Email: rjones@moriseiki.com
www.moriseikius.com/msu

Chapter 4

Veronika Noize

THE INTERVIEW

David Wright (Wright)

Today we're talking with Veronika (Ronnie) Noize, known as the SOHO Marketing Guru. Ronnie is the author of *How to Create a Killer Elevator Speech*, and *The Real Magic Bullet of Marketing*. As a marketing executive, she launched more than two hundred consumer products including software, books, comics, CDs, toys, and games, generating more than $650,000,000 in sales. Voted the 2007 Coach of the Year by her chapter of the International Coach Federation, and named one of the 100 Most Powerful Women by the NW Women's Journal, Ronnie is a dynamic speaker and much sought-after marketing expert who helps small office and home office (SOHO) businesses attract more clients.

Welcome to *Marketing Strategies*.

Veronika Noize (Noize)

Thank you, David; I'm looking forward to chatting with you.

Wright

What is the best marketing strategy that you have ever used to build your business?

Noize

Thank you for asking me my favorite question ever! The best marketing strategy that I've ever used to build my own business is one that I always recommend to my clients, and I call it my 30-Minute Networking Secret. It's my own take on a very focused networking process that teaches business professionals to refer to each other in a very short length of time. Not only is it amazingly effective, but it is flexible and appropriate for virtually any new business owner.

That's because being successful in business is less about having all the answers yourself than knowing where you can access expertise. Since you can't know everyone, you often rely on your friends or trusted colleagues for referrals, which is where your professional network comes in handy.

After all, a basic truth of business is that people do business with people they know, like, and trust. Happily, this model works both ways. The more people who know you or about you, the more business will come your way.

If we understand that each of us probably knows about two hundred other people well enough to call or e-mail them, doesn't it make sense that if we tapped into those individuals within our social and professional networks, we would have all the business we could handle? And even better, the leads would come to us predisposed to buy because they had been referred by a mutual acquaintance. So for me—a basically lazy person—networking was the easy route to success.

Wright

So how does your thirty-minute networking secret work?

Noize

It works very well! As a process, it is both simple and elegant. Basically, it is a thirty-minute meeting between two people in which both parties explain exactly how to refer clients to each other. Now that probably sounds ridiculously easy, but the reality is that most people have a lot of trouble explaining exactly who is their ideal client or prospect, so what should take seconds usually ends up taking twenty minutes or more.

You might think that would be a bad thing, but it isn't. As a matter of fact, I found it to be an advantage because the less time I had to talk during the meeting, the clearer my message needed to be, and the clearer my message was, the easier it was for the other person to understand and remember it. Bottom line: this means more referrals, better referrals, and as a bonus, a reputation for knowing what I am talking about, which is a good thing for business.

Wright

How did you develop this strategy?

Noize

What happened was that after I had been a successful marketing consultant for a few years, I completed my professional coach training. Delighted with the new coaching approach to working with clients, I wrapped up all my consulting contracts and was looking forward to spending my time coaching rather than consulting.

One bright and sunny Monday morning I entered my comfortable home office as usual, excited because this was the day I was to begin my career as a coach. In eager anticipation I sat down at my desk, and turned to my calendar for a preview of the day to come. My excitement flagged immediately when I looked closely at my calendar and realized that I hadn't yet booked any coaching clients.

Undaunted by my empty schedule, I asked myself what I would suggest a client do in this situation. Taking my own advice, I reviewed my marketing plan, noticing that I had planned to uncover leads for my coaching practice by networking. Disappointingly enough, the meetings I planned to attend weren't scheduled during the next two weeks. I looked around my desk for inspiration and found it in a stack of sixty-three business cards I had collected over the past year or so from attending various meetings.

Those sixty-three business cards, stacked in a small pile on my desk, reminded me of a new style of networking I had been wanting to test drive—a hybrid of Thomas Leonard's Team 100 concept and a one-on-one networking process I had used to my advantage in the past. In my mind I called it my "30-Minute Networking Secret," but aloud I referred to it as Thomas had: the Team 100.

So I set up sixty-three meetings over the course of six weeks, drank a lot of coffee, and learned to appreciate decaf. Naturally, after the first two weeks and twenty-one meetings, I was a bit worried. Not much had happened, but I was confident that the process would work—and it did.

Wright

What happened?

Noize

After two weeks and about twenty-one meetings I was tired, and a bit discouraged, but I knew that everything has a natural gestation period, so I knew that I needed to trust the process, and keep doing what I was doing. Am I glad I did!

After six weeks and sixty-three meetings, I had twenty-nine clients! Twenty-eight of those clients were referrals and one was from the group of sixty-three. Later, more of the sixty-three became clients, but at first, just that one.

Wright

What is a "Team 100"?

Noize

First, it is important to note that I learned of the Team 100 concept from Thomas Leonard, who was the founder of Coach U and CoachVille. He is widely recognized as one of the founders of the professional coaching industry. An article about Thomas and the coaching industry had caught my attention two years earlier, and that was the beginning of my journey into coaching.

I will explain a Team 100 as Thomas explained it to me. A Team 100 is a group of one hundred people with whom you have a professional relationship, either as a colleague, vendor, or client. Each of them has expertise in various areas.

A Team 100 can fill several functions in building your business: it can help develop into a strong professional network, allow you to tap in to expertise and knowledge, help you resolve problems or at least point toward someone who might help you, and of course, provide referrals to you. The relationship is reciprocal—members of your team get as much value from the relationship as you expect to get. You provide the same services to your contacts (your Team 100 members), thereby continuing the flow of support, advice, and leads.

To create the Team 100, Thomas suggested setting up lunch meetings on a weekly basis so that in the course of a couple of years, one would have a full one hundred other professionals who were also referral partners.

As a brand new coach with no clients, I didn't have the budget (although I did have the time) to set up a series of expensive lunches. I also discovered that people were less and less open to longer "get-to-know-you meetings," but responded really well to the referral part of the Team 100 model, so that became my focus. And frankly, I did not want to spend the time over a lengthy lunch when my objectives could be met with a simple thirty-minute meeting over coffee.

With such a short meeting, I had to come up with a few questions that would give me a clear idea of how to refer, and that I could answer quickly, because I found out early that most people preferred to talk rather than listen in these meetings.

Wright

What did you bring to the Team 100 concept?

Noize

My contributions to the Team 100 process as I use it today are as follows:

First, I clarified the purpose of my Team 100 as a referral mechanism. I decided that I didn't want people calling on me for free information and services, so I would not expect that from those on my team. My sole purpose in creating the team would be to connect to others in order to serve others because there is tremendous value in being able to offer qualified leads and referrals to those in my network. This networking process creates a solid network of people to whom I can refer with confidence (since I've personally met with them and understand who their ideal clients are) and who can do the same for me.

Second, I codified a list of three critical questions to ask during the meetings. Recognizing that most people would not know how to teach me to refer to them in an organized fashion, I asked myself what I would need to know to refer to them with confidence. The three questions that form the basis of the meeting are:

- Who is your ideal client or the perfect referral for you?
- How will I recognize that person?
- What do you want me to tell that person when I refer him or her to you?

Third, I prepared a script for inviting others to meet with me. This was one of the most important aspects of the meeting because the success of each meeting depended on the expectations set for the meeting. A meeting in which the expectations were not met was a disaster, but a meeting that met or exceeded expectations was a success. The expectations were simple:

- We would meet at a coffee shop.
- We would spend just thirty minutes.
- We would teach each other how best to refer to us.

Wright
Why do you think your process work so well?

Noize
There are several factors that make my version of the process work exceptionally well. But before I explain why I think it works, I should mention that I tried to do the Team 100 process in the way that Thomas originally explained it: meet for lunch, over coffee, or at the other person's office for an hour or so, and to allow each of us the leisure of thirty minutes to talk about our respective businesses.

I discovered very quickly that it was too expensive (in money, time, and energy) to meet for lunch. I also found that demanding equal time in the meeting often diminished the quality of referrals that I would get and that presenting my information in a certain way kept me from diluting my own message—it can be difficult for the untrained listener to pick out the most important points unless you are excruciatingly clear and brief.

That's what made me finally realize that by limiting my contributions to the conversation to the questions I asked, and a scant ninety seconds spent on answering the three critical questions, my message would be heard, understood, and remembered far better than if I spent thirty minutes discoursing at length.

And finally, meeting at a neutral place kept the meeting on an even footing, making me feel less like a beggar than like a professional with something to offer. Meetings held at either person's office seemed to tilt the balance of power in such a way that made the mutual benefit of the meeting seem too uneven. For example, the few meetings I held that took place in the other persons' offices were interrupted by phone calls, other people, and even by e-mail, which made me feel more like a job applicant than a professional setting up an alliance.

Even though I know that the folks I met with at their offices were sincere in wanting to form the alliance, their lack of attention to our meeting (or perhaps I should say their attention to the interruptions) offended me and made me less disposed to refer to them. Why did it offend me? Because my time is worth something, and by agreeing to meet for our mutual benefit, there was an expectation set that I felt was not met—an expectation of courtesy, attention to the conversation at hand, and understanding of the value of the alliance.

But bad meetings were really anomalous in my experience; most of the thirty-minute meetings went really well.

What works about my process is that the bulk of the thirty minutes are devoted solely to learning how to refer to someone else. Just imagine how you would feel if someone took the time out of his or her busy schedule to sit down with you, focus on finding out who would be the best referral for you, and asked you what could be said in the referral process that would help the person being referred understand why you're a good choice! In some ways, it might feel like it was almost too good to be true, wouldn't it? But in our information-overloaded world, where we can connect electronically with just about anyone at any time, it seems to me that the personal touch is often missing. Seeing someone across the table who is listening intently to what you are saying, taking notes, and asking questions without demanding an equal share of the conversation is about as rare as the dodo bird these days.

I found that most people were delighted to open up, explore the topic of who their ideal clients and prospects were, and really be heard while they were talking about themselves and their business.

But you know, as great as all that stuff is, that's probably not really why the process works. I believe that the process works because when we focus on service, rather than scramble for dollars, we attract clients like magnets. Our willingness to serve others makes others more willing to help us, and so everybody benefits. The referrer looks good because he or she has the ability to offer a resource to the referred, who is looking for help. The person receiving the referral gets the business, so everybody's a winner.

Wright

It sounds great, but a little overwhelming. Isn't it a lot of time?

Noize

Creating an extensive professional network is not nearly as time-consuming or intimidating as you might think, but it does take conscious effort. I call my network my "Team 100" but of course, you can call yours whatever you like.

Deliberate, organized networking can be one of the strongest lead generators for any service-related business, as well as many consumer and business products businesses, and I have found that thirty-minute networking meetings work like magic for me. That's because networking is more than facetime—it's about really getting to know others. And most people make one of two mistakes when they're networking: doing too much or doing too little.

Doing too much networking means attending meeting after meeting, but failing to really connect with other people in a meaningful way. Just showing up at networking meetings isn't enough; you need to spend some time getting to know other people, learning about their businesses, and understanding how (and who) to refer to those folks, just as you are hoping they will do for you.

Doing too little networking means joining groups but not attending meetings or attending meetings but not interacting with others in the group. Just being on a membership roster isn't networking, and if you really want to network, you have to be prepared to step out of your shell and actually talk with other people.

Wright

Can we move back to your three questions?

Noize

There are three questions that will elicit the type of information you need to be able to refer business appropriately:

1. Who is your ideal client, the perfect referral to you?

The sad truth is that a lot of people will tell you that anyone with a credit card and a pulse is a good referral, but that's not going to work, for a number of reasons. Ask for both demographic and psychographic info here. If the person just says something general, gently press for more specifics or ask for a description of the perfect client for his or her business. If this question doesn't get much of a response, ask hypothetical questions such as: If you could clone just one of your clients, who would it be, and why? What is it that makes this particular client so good for your business?

2. How will I recognize that client?

You may need to probe here, such as asking if there is a situation, such as divorce, inheritance, or opening a new business that is present in your ideal clients' lives. Or is there a certain phrase that clients often use, such as being overwhelmed or needing help with something specific that you should listen for?

3. What would you like me to tell any referrals about you when I give them your contact information?

This could be anything: you've never lost a case or your clients usually get a 100 percent return on their investment within thirty days. You could give personal information such as you're a classically trained pianist in addition to being a jazz composer or that you come from a spiritual base. This is your opportunity to include some significant information about yourself or your practice that will resonate with your ideal client.

Of course, most people will want you to say that they're the best (which you probably can't say from experience) or they might even want you to do some selling for them, but that's not the point. The point is to offer one tidbit of information that is helpful to the person looking for help, so he or she can feel reassured that this person might really have the answers.

Wright
How did you make sure you were asked the right questions?

Noize

For me, it was easy because I created a sheet for notes (this is available on my Web site for free). I call it my "Team 100 Notes sheet." What I would do is take notes while interviewing the other person, after first asking permission, of course. Taking notes demonstrated my preparation and focused agenda of understanding exactly how I could refer with confidence.

By having a set of specific questions to ask, rather than just making up something on the fly, I had a script to follow, thus moving the conversation along the right track in a timely manner.

Having an extra Team 100 Notes sheet to give to the other person was really handy, too. I discovered almost immediately that most people would come to the meeting with no paper, so having an extra sheet was helpful to them, and gave me the opportunity to answer the questions I wanted them to ask me.

I found that the act of writing down information helps lodge it firmly in our memories, and if you want the other person to ask you the questions you are prepared to answer, and to remember your responses, you need to be prepared. So I was and I found that nobody refused the notes sheet when I offered it.

Since I knew the questions in advance, I was prepared to give my answers quickly—usually in about ninety seconds. Many times these meetings will focus more on the other person for the first twenty to twenty-five minutes, but that doesn't mean that you can't get your point across when it's your turn to answer questions. You know the questions before the meeting, so you can be prepared to give clear, concise, and memorable responses to the questions when you're asked, even with only five minutes to spare.

Wright

What about writing down the answers on your notes sheet for the other person in advance?

Noize

Even though that sounds like the ultimate in preparedness, it is just not a good idea at all. Here's the reason: you want the other person to listen to your answers, write down your key points, and ideally, keep the paper. But even if that piece of paper is tossed in the garbage can on the way out, if what you said was written down, the other person heard who to refer to you, what to listen for, and how to refer to you very clearly. By writing your information, it was heard, seen, and felt, so it is logical to believe it will be remembered.

You deprive the person of the chance to remember your message if you clutter it up with too much information or if he or she doesn't get the opportunity to interact with it, such as writing it down.

Wright

What if the other person is not a good prospect; should I even bother meeting?

Noize

Yes! Meet with as many people as you can. Not every person you meet is a prospect, but nearly every person you meet can be a valuable part of your network. Remember, we all know about two hundred people we can refer, so every person you meet with is a connection to others, just as you are a connection to your network for him or her.

And just because someone isn't a prospect right now doesn't mean the person won't be in the future. And once you have people's trust, they'll be able to refer others in their circle of influence to you.

Wright

What if the other person is a good prospect; can the meeting morph into a sales presentation?

Noize

Of course, there is always the possibly that others will recognize themselves in your ideal client description and will want to talk to you in more detail. Although it will be very tempting to extend this meeting and turn it to your advantage this way, <u>don't do it</u>. If the other person really is a prospect, you can set up another time to chat so that your meeting will have a different agenda than networking. If you don't do this, you will be remembered as someone who "baited and switched" that person into a meeting. Bad karma, I'm telling you!

Set up another meeting after your Team 100 meeting if you get the chance, but don't allow the Team 100 meeting to turn into an immediate sales opportunity because that is not what you promised when you set up the meeting.

Wright

What is the best way to refer?

Noize

There are many ways to share referrals, and the situation decrees which is best. Here are the three ways that I find I use the most:

The first and most obvious way to share referrals is in response to the question, "Do you know anyone who could help me do/get/be _____?" or, "Do you know a good_____?" In this case, assuming I know at least one person, I say yes, and either give that person's business card (if I have it), or e-mail that person's contact information. I always ask if the person I am referring wants me to copy the person I am referring him or her to on the e-mail so the person will expect a call or perhaps even take the initiative by making contact.

Another great way to give referrals is when you know someone is in need or would be open to a suggestion; you can simply refer to the appropriate person. In my Team 100 meetings, I ask my referral partners what to listen for in conversation and what to say when I refer. Since I ask such specific questions, I'm able to uncover the best referrals for others.

Because listening for something specific makes it so easy to recognize a referral opportunity, I appreciate knowing exactly what to listen for. Now when I hear people complain about how they hate to get their picture taken, for example, I know that's my cue to refer them to a certain photographer in my Team 100. This particular photographer has also given me a stack of promo postcards, so I can just pop one in the mail, which makes referring to her so quick and easy.

The third way is to send out a message to the people in my network telling them about a great experience I just had with no other agenda than to spread the good word about someone I'm happy to recommend. This is great because it usually sparks some business for the person I'm commending, even when I didn't know if anyone else could use his or her services.

Of course, there are many other ways to refer, but these are my current favorites.

Wright

Who are the best people to have in a referral list?

Noize

Although it is very handy to have a wide variety of occupations, talents, and areas of expertise on your referral list, the ones you will probably refer to most often are professionals who serve the same clientele as you do, and who offer complimentary services.

For example, as we work together, my clients create marketing plans that frequently include such useful tools as business cards, newsletters, Web sites, and other marketing materials. For that very reason, I have a number of copywriters, graphic artists, SEO experts, and other marketing services providers such as Web hosts, newsletter services, printers, and so on.

Since some of my clients are in start-up mode, I've got a list of business resources to refer to as well, including lawyers, bookkeepers, accountants, and commercial realtors. It has also been very timely to have image-related professionals on my Team 100—image consultants, photographers, hair stylists, and tailors.

Another category of service providers I have found essential on my list is marketing consultants and coaches. This might seem counterintuitive to include my "competition," doesn't it? But the truth is that no matter how hard I work, I will never be able to serve all the people who need services like mine, nor would I want to because my approach, personality, and style are not right for everyone. For that reason alone, it has been extremely helpful to me to be able to refer to others.

My goal is to serve every person who comes to me for help and sometimes the best way I can serve is to refer to another marketing coach or consultant.

Wright

Where can potential referral partners be found?

Noize

Finding potential referral partners is easier than you might imagine! You can start by looking through your own personal database of contacts, including family members, friends, neighbors, people in your church, neighborhood association, parent/teacher association, special interest or hobby group, networking meetings, trade or industry associations, and so on.

After you've connected with the people you already know in those organizations (and most people have about two hundred people who fall in those categories), you can branch out by introducing yourself to the people in those groups whom you don't yet know.

The next step is to brainstorm a list of other service providers or retailers who also serve your client base. Since two heads are often better than one, sit down with your coach, a colleague, or a friend to brainstorm. Ask yourself who your ideal client needs to see before the person works with you, what the person's options are for your type of service or product (because no matter what you offer, there are always other options), and what he or she needs to do after you.

To get referrals, you have to figure out who your client needs before working with them. And believe it or not, you may also have an opportunity to refer to that person as well. Often clients do not do things in the correct order and you want to be of service to your prospects and clients; no matter where they are in the process.

The reason you want to figure out who your client needs after you is to help your client, and to offer referrals to others.

Wright

Let's back up a bit to a question I know will be on our readers' minds: what did you say—exactly—to set up these meetings?

Noize

What you say to set up meetings will depend on your relationship to the person. You would probably say one thing to someone you've known for a long time, and something slightly different to a person you've never met but want to meet to develop a mutually beneficial relationship.

Here is one short script that I've used to set up meetings:

"Hi David, this is Ronnie Noize. We met briefly last month at the XYZ meeting, and I am the gal who sat at the table up front. Is this a good time for a quick chat?"

If he says yes, then I will say, "Great! David, I was just looking at your business card and I was thinking that I probably know some folks who would be good prospects for you, but to tell the truth, I don't know for sure. Would you be willing to meet me for a half hour next week and bring me up to speed on what makes the best referral for you? Afterward, I can share what makes a good referral for me. Sound okay?"

If the answer is yes, I say something like, "Thanks! How about meeting at the coffee shop on 19th and Vine? When would be a good time for you?"

"Okay, we're all set. See you next Thursday!"

Wright

Sounds easy enough, but did you ever make a cold call to set up a meeting?

Noize

Yes, and some of those "cold calls" turned out to be some of my best referral partners! The reason the cold calls worked for me is that I was completely honest with the people I called, letting them know that I was impressed by their reputation or how I found them or whatever, and that I needed to have them in my network.

The majority of the people I've cold-called to meet with were favorably impressed by my initiative and liked the idea of creating the referral alliance with a qualified professional, so what started as a cold call ended up as a warm relationship.

Wright

Have you ever met with anyone you didn't like?

Noize

Yes, although I didn't know it when the meeting was arranged. Life is too short to accept meetings with people I don't like, but when the acquaintance is new, I might not realize that I'm not a good fit with that person until we're at the table.

While the process of building a Team 100 is very solid, there can be the occasional hiccup in the system, particularly when you meet someone you don't like on a personal level or someone you don't trust for whatever reason. The ironic thing is that people I don't particularly like often like each other, so I do have some folks I refer to on such occasions.

For example, I worked with a woman once who disliked me on sight, and made her dislike obvious. Of course I was polite to her, even though I didn't care for her style either. We agreed that we weren't a good fit to work together, but I do respect her professional expertise, so from time to time I have referred to her.

She refers to me too, and I can easily identify her referrals because they all say the same thing: "She says that you really know your stuff, if I can 'stomach your personality.' She says she can't stand working with you, but she finds your Web site helpful, although your style is like fingernails on a chalkboard to her."

Wright

How did you stay in touch after the meeting?

Noize

Staying in touch is really important to keep the relationship alive. Following a networking meeting, I send a note of thanks, add that person to my mailing list, and then make a point of personally touching base every quarter or even every six months, depending on my schedule. Result: another resource for my professional network (I love to refer people!), plus another person who knows, likes, and trusts me, and equally important, another person in my network who is now in the position to refer business (my ideal clients!) to me.

Part of maintaining your professional network is staying in touch, which you can do through notes, calls, invitations, and such, but the easiest way is probably through your newsletter. How can you offer to do that without sounding like you're selling something (not a way you want to end this meeting)? What I do is suggest that in order to stay in touch and updated about our respective businesses, we should add each other to our newsletter or mailing lists. The part about keeping updated about the businesses actually allows us to refer better, and removes the impression that we're trying to sell the other person.

Wright

Any final words of advice for those considering using your thirty-minute networking secret strategy to build business fast?

Noize

Yes! Understand that these things take time! When I first used this process, I was disappointed that after two weeks nothing had happened, but I kept the faith and persevered. It paid off in a big way and continues to pay off to this day.

Also understand that this is a reciprocal process and that you must give to receive the full benefit. I make it a point not to keep score, because that's counterproductive.

If I only referred to those who referred to me, I would have had to wait a long time for any referrals. I prefer to help the referee (the person I refer) to get the help, support, or services they need, and the person I refer to benefits from the referral. When everybody wins, the process works.

About the Author

VERONIKA (RONNIE) NOIZE, known as the SOHO Marketing Guru, is the author of *How to Create a Killer Elevator Speech*, and *The Real Magic Bullet of Marketing*. As a marketing executive, she launched more than two hundred consumer products including software, books, comics, CDs, toys, and games, generating more than $650,000,000. Voted the 2007 Coach of the Year by her chapter of the International Coach Federation, and named one of the 100 Most Powerful Women by the *NW Women's Journal*, Ronnie is a dynamic speaker and sought-after marketing expert who helps small businesses attract more clients through her presentations, products, and programs.

Veronika Noize
SOHO Marketing Guru Business Coaching & Development LLC
1305 Columbia Street, Suite 250
Vancouver, WA 98660
Phone: 360.882.1298
E-mail: Ronnie@VeronikaNoize.com
www.SOHOMarketingGuru.com

Chapter 5

Michael G. Cannon

David E. Wright (Wright)

Today we're talking with Michael Cannon, a respected sales and marketing effectiveness expert and CEO of Silver Bullet Group. Numerous studies and statistics bear out that companies lose billions of dollars each year because of ineffective messaging. Some of the factors that contribute to this messaging mess are that most companies, and the marketing firms that support them, do not have an objective set of criteria to evaluate messaging quality prior to market testing or launch. They also do not have a process or the skills that they need in order to create high-quality messaging. What is the impact? Sales and marketing effectiveness is reduced by about 25% and costs U.S. companies alone over $100 billion every year.

Michael's 20 years of sales, marketing, and management experience in many different industries led him to create the Silver Bullet Sales Messaging System™, a proven, proprietary methodology for helping B2B companies dramatically improve the quality of their messaging and significantly increase their revenues, marketshare, and profits. Michael has assisted hundreds of companies to increase revenues up to 1,300%! Michael was featured on the front cover of *Self-Employed America* magazine and has addressed numerous audiences around the world, including *Entrepreneur Magazine Sales and Marketing Radio Show*, the American Marketing Association, and Vistage International.

Michael, welcome to our *Marketing Strategies That Really Work* interview. I'm excited to learn more about your sales messaging system and how it's worked for your clients.

Michael G. Cannon (Cannon)
Thanks, David. Fire away!

Wright
How would you describe the way U.S. companies address problems with their sales and marketing effectiveness today?

Cannon
David, when companies are not meeting their revenue and profit goals, the finger-pointing begins and it almost always points in one direction first: the sales team. The company's management team seems to consistently find different ways to say, "The problem is not the company, the market, the products, or the marketing. We just need better, more effective sales or business development people." This thinking puts into motion what I call the "fire, hire, and repeat" strategy — it's the perfect fodder for a Dilbert cartoon strip. To fix the lagging sales problem, a portion of the sales team is fired, a new team is hired and trained, and some 6 to 12 months later, if sales are still lagging, the spotlight and the firing and hiring shift to sales management, and if that doesn't improve things, the VP of Sales is next in line, proceeding all the way up to CEO if there is no improvement.

This fire-hire-and-repeat strategy is quite familiar to most of us business warriors. Yet, anyone who has been on the front line also knows that throwing new sales people into a company or product line that is not meeting its revenue goals rarely remedies the situation. This is because the sales people are usually not the main problem. In my observations, it's usually the system that supports — or fails to support — the sales team that is the real problem. Examples that the sales support system is broken include market research from the American Marketing Association's Customer Message Management Forums, which a few years ago discovered a startling statistic: "80 to 90 percent of marketing collateral is considered useless by Sales." Interestingly enough, this comes as no surprise to most marketing professionals. According to a recent poll that appeared in *BtoB* magazine, some 70 percent of marketers polled gave themselves "D's" and "F's" on the quality and effectiveness of their sales support messaging and materials. So throwing new sales people into a broken sales support system makes little sense and it's terribly expensive and time-consuming. As a strategy, "fire, hire, and repeat" is a major drain on productivity, profits, and morale, and it has a very negative impact on any company's ability to stay competitive.

Wright

So, what should they do instead?

Cannon

Since we are discussing messaging as a strategy to improve sales and marketing effectiveness, I'm going to assume a few things, such as: the business model is correct, there is a logical alignment between the offering and the target market, the "go to" market plan makes sense, and the product is not defective. Given that these important fundamentals are in place, I think the answer is that companies must focus on building a solid sales support infrastructure or system that is capable of creating and enabling a high-performing sales team.

Several components make up this system:

- It includes having the appropriate positions, like inside versus outside sales or farmers versus hunters, plus the associated job descriptions and compensation plans defined and aligned with company objectives and market requirements.
- It includes a hiring process that identifies competent salespeople, which means it needs to include a structured interview process and profiling or testing for the right skills, aptitude, and personality.
- It includes a formal sales process or a set of best practices that is used to create leads, meetings, buying events, and orders.
- It includes reports that track the sales activities, goals, and processes, and distinguish pipeline from forecast.
- It ensures that the management team is effective in terms of providing coaching, accountability, and recognition.

- It includes the providing of training in the areas of product and sales enablement, as well as traditional sales skills training.
- It includes collateral and sales tools that are synchronized and that support the key steps in the sales processes.
- And, of course, it includes high-quality messaging that is used across all the customer touch points, collateral, and sales tools.

Experience has shown that focusing on the creation of a solid sales support infrastructure, as I have just defined it, is essential to achieving and exceeding revenue, marketshare, and profit targets, and I'm convinced that great messaging, and specifically great sales messaging, is one of the most critical components for building a successful sales support infrastructure.

Wright

I've certainly heard a lot about "brand messaging" and "product messaging" over the years, but what exactly is "*sales* messaging"?

Cannon

Let me answer that by first providing a definition for messaging, which is, quite simply, the words you use, both written and verbal, to convince a prospective customer to do business with your firm. Most messaging, like brand messaging, company messaging, product messaging, and even most value propositions, in my observation, are descriptive. They provide a description of what your company does, the products and services you offer, the features of each offering, and, if done well, a little bit about the benefits of your offering and the benefits of doing business with your company.

Great sales messaging on the other hand is persuasive. It provides compelling and persuasive answers to your buyer's primary buying questions, such as "Why should I meet with you?" and "Why should I change out my current solution for a new solution?" and "Why should I buy this solution from you?", for each product or service your company offers.

A key point I want to make here is that companies need both descriptive messaging and persuasive messaging to be successful. The problem is that most companies primarily provide descriptive messaging. I think they are making this mistake because they do not know what sales messaging is. They also don't know how sales messaging is different from the other messaging types they create and they don't know how to use great sales messaging as a tool to improve messaging effectiveness.

Wright

I notice that you always include the word "great" to describe sales messaging. How would you define "great sales messaging?"

Cannon

Let me share with you some of the principles that make sales messaging great.

1) First, **great sales messaging is aligned with the product life cycle and the types of buying questions prospects ask as they go through their buying process.** For example, when you go through the car-buying process — which is a mature product — you ask yourself a series of questions that go something like this: Do I want to buy a new car? What type of car do I want to buy? Whom am I going to buy the car from?

There are similar buying questions that must be answered for each product as it goes through the product life cycle. For example, in the early stages of a product's life cycle the most important buyer question is likely to be "Why should I change out my current solution for a new solution?". The answer to this question has little to do with your company, per se. The primary goal of your sales messaging, at this early stage, is to create *demand* by stating *a compelling reason to change*, convincing buyers that there is great value to be gained in changing from their current solution to a new or better solution.

In the late-market stage of a product's life cycle, when marketing demand is more established, the primary buying question becomes "Why should I buy *your* solution rather than a competitor's?". The answer to this question must focus on competitive differentiation. The primary goal of your sales messaging, at this later stage of a product's life cycle, is to create *a compelling reason to buy the solution from your company* rather than from the competition, meaning that you want to create orders for your company.

2) A second principle is that **great sales messaging must be specific to one offering**, that is, you need to have specific sales messaging for each offering or product or service bundle that you sell.

3) Another principle is that **great sales messaging must be comparative**. This may seem self-evident, yet a lot of messaging does not manifest this principle. When you are developing *demand*-creation messaging, it's not about the value of your solution. It's about *the value of the difference between your solution and the customer's current solution*. On the other hand, when you're developing *order*-creation messaging or competitive messaging, it's not about the value of your solution. It's about *the value of the difference between your solution and the competitors' solutions*. The operating principle is that if you can help buyers solve their problems or reach their objectives better than their current solution and better than the competition, then you should win the business.

4) A fourth principle is that **great sales messaging must be customer value-centric**. What I mean by this is that you can answer a buyer's questions at three different levels: a) Feature, b) Benefit, and c) Customer-Business Value. The difference between feature, benefit, and customer-business value is the difference between a "so what," a "nice to have," and a "compelling reason to buy!" Or, to put a visual spin on it, it's the difference between *a drill, a hole in the ground*, and *an oil well*. What the buyers really want to buy or what they value, I think, is the oil well.

5) The fifth principle that I want to talk about is that **great sales messaging must provide proof points, such as customer testimonials and case studies**. In a buyer's eyes, a company's messaging is viewed as a claim and treated with skepticism, but when the same messaging is quoted from a customer, then the messaging is perceived as more likely to be true.

These are just a few of the principles of great sales messaging, and when a company develops and deploys its own sales messaging program that adheres to these principles, the impact on sales and marketing effectiveness is astounding.

Wright

Michael, I'm curious, how did you personally arrive at "sales messaging" as being a key piece of the solution to increasing sales and marketing effectiveness? Was it a bolt out of the blue? Or the end result of years of experience?

Cannon

Both, actually. That "ah ha" moment came through many years of experience. I was fortunate enough to be promoted into sales management fairly early in my career — by the age of 25 I was managing a sales team of over 30 people. My sales management philosophy was, and still is, that the job of salespeople is to make or exceed their quota. My job was to do what I could to make it easier for them to hit their numbers. This approach created what I humorously called my nights-and-weekends job, meaning that during the day we were focused on driving deals into and through the sales funnel, and in my spare time I was focused on creating the sales support infrastructure needed to improve the sales team's effectiveness.

When you spend a lot of time thinking about all the tools the sales team needs to become more effective and then prioritize that list, what you will find over time is that having a compelling answer to why prospects should meet with you, change out their current solution, or buy your product over the competition's is absolutely critical. You don't get very far without those answers, so it's vital that compelling answers to these questions are developed and incorporated into almost every sales process and tool.

Also, I noticed over time that my sales teams were consistently being rewarded with president's club-type trips, so I just kept adhering to my approach with my sales teams. I was famous for saying, "We need some 'silver bullets' to win this account or grow revenues." Over time, I learned that this was my way of saying "value proposition." Once I was able to consciously put a name to that aspect of what I was doing, I started to focus more of my time on how to create the best "silver bullets" or value propositions for my sales team.

Over the years, that quest led me to the concept of sales messaging, the principles of *great* sales messaging, and the perfecting of a process for developing and deploying great sales messaging, or "silver bullets" as I still like to call them. It's been so rewarding to see firsthand the power of "great sales messaging" as companies integrate it into their marketing and sales programs. I guess you could liken my "ah ha" moment to all those Hollywood actors who are "overnight successes" after years and years of concentrated effort developing their craft.

Wright

So when a company comes to you for assistance in solving its sales and revenue problems, how do you help them determine if they have a messaging problem?

Cannon

Well, David, the first step to solving any problem is realizing you have one to begin with and then making sure you identify it correctly. Many companies struggling to make their revenue and profit goals think they know what the problem is and many of them are wrong. If a company is not meeting or exceeding its revenue and marketshare objectives or its new product introductions are not meeting revenue projections, one of the first questions to ask is, "Do we have the messaging right?". To help answer the question, I recommend doing one or more of the following audits: a sales collateral audit, a messaging audit, a field sales time use audit, and/or a field/channel training audit.

The *sales collateral audit* will help you determine what percentage of your collateral is not considered useful in helping Sales generate revenue. Does your company's collateral fall into that 80 to 90 percent of marketing collateral mentioned earlier that sales groups across the country consider useless? Is your marketing group part of that 70 percent of marketeers who give themselves failing grades in the materials they provide to Sales? If more than 20 percent of the collateral fails the usefulness test, it's likely you have a messaging problem.

Another way to determine if you have the right messaging is by conducting a *messaging audit*. Our research indicates that U.S. companies alone waste more than $100 billion every year confusing sales messaging with other messaging types. To do a messaging audit, you identify the buyer's key buying question and then evaluate your current messaging. How well does your messaging answer the buyer's question? How many of the principles of great sales messaging does the answer incorporate? It's critical that companies provide compelling answers to their buyer's questions, and we covered some of the key buying questions earlier when I was outlining some of the principles of great sales messaging.

If your collateral and messaging are not good, then a *field sales time use audit* will show that your field sales teams are spending a lot of selling time creating their own collateral and messaging — materials they feel they need to meet their sales objectives and that they aren't getting from Marketing. This problem is supported by a recent report from the Aberdeen Group, which stated that "salespeople spend typically 30 to 50 hours each month searching for information and recreating customer-facing content." We all know that sales reps are revenue optimization machines, meaning, their objective is to do the least amount of work for the most amount of revenue. So, if your reps are spending any time creating customer-facing messaging and materials, then the reason they are doing it is because they need those materials in order to close deals. I think it's much more effective to have one marketing person create the messaging and collateral, and then leverage that work over your entire sales team.

The last audit I want to mention is the *field/channel training audit*. What percentage of the sales team feels the new product training is useful in helping it effectively sell the product? The same question applies to competitive training and training on specific market opportunities. There is typically great friction in these training areas, between Sales who receives the training and Marketing who creates and delivers the training. How on earth can Sales be effective at selling if it does not understand the product in the context of how it helps customers solve meaningful problems and how it helps generate meaningful business value? Improving messaging quality has proven to be quite effective in connecting these data points and reducing the friction between these teams.

Wright

Once a company buys into the idea that it has a messaging problem and that great sales messaging might just be the key element to boosting its sales, what's the next step?

Cannon

The best way to improve messaging quality is to employ the four steps in the Silver Bullet Sales Messaging System.

The first step is for you to **identify the prospect's primary buying questions**, such as "Why should I change out my current solution for a new solution?", "Why should I buy your solution rather than a competitive offering?", and "Why should I meet or talk with you?".

In the second step, you **identify improvements to the customer's condition** employing the Use Case Methodology, which compares what a customer's condition was like both before and after using the company's product or service or as compared to using the competition's product or service. You must understand the value of the difference in order to create great messaging.

In the third step, you **answer the prospect's buying questions**. You do this by composing persuasive and compelling answers by creating three to five value statements that appeal to the buyer's emotional reasons for buying and that provide an intellectual justification for the decision. Then you develop a meaningful list of evidence and proof to back up the claims and summarize the answers on a single page.

The last step is to **deploy your sales messaging for optimal results**. There are many ways to leverage your new sales messaging. For example, you can:

- Create a section in your online content and printed product brochure called "Three Great Reasons to Replace Your Current Solution or Three Great Reasons to Select Us Over the Competition." Then provide your value statements, supporting points, and a link for readers to get more information.

- Use each value statement separately in an advertising or demand-generation campaign, with the goal of driving readers to a landing page where they can get more information.

- Create online and scripted demonstrations that illustrate how you deliver on each value statement.

- Incorporate your messaging into your field and channel product and competitive training programs.

- What you must do is leverage your sales messaging across all the potential customer touch points, collateral, and sales tools. It maximizes the return on your messaging improvement investment. *Create it once, use it everywhere!*

Wright

When companies invest in developing and implementing a sales messaging program, what can they expect in return?

Cannon

You know, I knew you were going to ask me this question, and I must say, I'm still a little reluctant to answer it, mainly because I'm concerned that the answer is just too amazing. So let's see what you think.

If we can agree that messaging is defined as the words you use, both written and verbal, to convince prospects to buy from your company, then, if you improve the quality of your messaging, you also improve the effectiveness of all your sales and marketing investments. That's the strategy. You can make big improvements in the effectiveness of your sales and marketing teams simply by improving the quality of your messaging. And, what sales messaging does is give you an objective way to improve the quality of your messaging.

Think of it like this: Messaging is the fuel that powers your sales and marketing engines. When you improve the quality of the fuel, that is, boost the fuel's octane level, for example, you improve the effectiveness of your sales and marketing engines. What sales messaging does is boost the octane level of the fuel, which improves the effectiveness — think return on investment — of all your sales and marketing engines, often by 30 percent or more in just a few quarters.

It's a simple marketing strategy with huge implications. Let me give you a sense for just how big an impact the addition of sales messaging can have on your sales and marketing teams. In fact, let's look at it from several different perspectives: your company, your direct field sales/sales operations/channel teams, and your product management/product marketing teams.

From the *company* perspective, the impact of adding sales messaging is that:

- It increases competitiveness.
- It increases revenues and marketshare.
- And it increases profits.

Sales messaging quite literally improves many of the key company metrics that matter to the Board and the CEO.

The impact of adding sales messaging for the *direct field sales* team is that:

- It increases the size of the sales pipeline.
- It improves the win/loss ratio, or the proposal-to-order ratio.
- It increases the average order size.
- And it reduces discounting.

The result of implementing sales messaging for the *sales operations* team is that:

- It increases the effectiveness of the product training, competitive training, and traditional sales skills training for both direct and partner sales channels.
- It increases time-to-channel effectiveness by reducing the amount of time it takes the field to successfully start selling a new product.
- And it increases sales capacity, which is the percentage of the sales team that can effectively sell a product.

The impact of adding sales messaging for the *channel sales* team is just as profound in that:

- All the performance improvements that we discussed regarding the field sales team also apply to the channel sales team, with the net effect that channel partner sales and revenues increase, too!
- It also increases the number of channel partners.

The marketing department is also a significant beneficiary. The value to the *product management* team in implementing sales messaging is that:

- It increases customer focus, meaning that there is better alignment of new product investment with the solving of valuable customer problems.
- It results in more competitive products.
- And it results in higher margins.

The impact on the *product marketing* team when they implement sales messaging is that:

- It increases the percentage of deliverables (that is, training, collateral, and sales tools) considered useful to helping sales generate revenue.
- It increases Marketing's ability to market solutions.
- And it creates faster penetration of new and existing markets.

This is why the answer is so hard to believe, David. It's so simple yet so powerful. Improve your messaging and you make dramatic improvements in the effectiveness of all your sales and marketing investments. It truly is the Holy Grail or "silver bullet" for increasing revenues, profits, and marketshare.

Oh, and one more point, great sales messaging can do all this for a company, plus everyone makes more commissions and bonuses and they enjoy their jobs more. It's such a powerful and exciting strategy. OK, I'll stand down. What do you think?

Wright

Wow…it seems like people would have to seriously consider this idea as a strategic initiative for their companies. In order for you to bring these points to life, I was wondering if you could share a few of the successes that have happened after your client companies have embraced your sales messaging system. What proof do you have that these improvements can be realized?

Cannon

David, let me start with some recent market research and then give you some case studies.

According to a recent CSO Insights study, companies that describe themselves as world-class in terms of consistent customer [sales] messaging that they've provided effectively to Sales and with collateral driven by market segments and customer needs:

- Outpaced other firms in quota achievement by 25 percent.
- Had win rates that were 20 percent higher.
- Were three times more successful in proposal closing.
- And were five times better at eliminating excessive discounting.

Another survey conducted by Forrester in November 2006 found that companies are at least 6 times more likely to have a "best provider" relationship when they understand the business goals of the individual IT and business stakeholders and can articulate the business value of their solutions in terms of how it impacts each stakeholder directly.

These reports provide some excellent substantiation of the impressive improvements that can be made and are in alignment with some of the improvements cited in Silver Bullet Group's case studies.

For example, Agilent Technologies' Electronic Measurement Group, or EMG, has significantly increased its competitiveness with a new program of competitive training and marketing materials. Agilent, which is a leading electronics and scientific measurement company, knew that its products were extremely competitive in what is regarded as a highly competitive market, yet the Field

Engineers, or FEs, who make up the EMG field sales team were finding it more and more difficult to win in those highly competitive sales situations. They complained that the competitive information was complex and hard to understand, plus it didn't communicate Agilent's excellent value propositions. Agilent knew it needed to make major improvements in the development, understanding, and dissemination of the EMG's competitive information.

Using the Silver Bullet Group Sales Messaging System, the marketing teams were able to better describe their product's competitive advantages and what those mean to the customer. They can now more readily describe how Agilent's equipment is better at solving customer problems than the competition and delivers better value. This deeper understanding of the customer's needs and the competition's capabilities also enables competitive claims to be countered effectively with factual, meaningful information.

The results of the rollout were rapid and compelling. As Product Sales Manager Nigel Mott reported, "Great sales messaging increased our products' win rate by 30 percent and reduced the time we spend supporting the field by around 50 percent for the product family I support." In the most recent internal poll, 56 percent of the field sales organization said that the quality of the new competitive intelligence enabled each of them to close at least one additional deal during the company's last quarter.

Today the EMG field sales team is winning against the competition more and more frequently. And the ease of use of these new, concise, fact-based tools has increased productivity, as well. It's a much happier sales staff. As Ed Sullivan, District Manager of Field Sales for the Americas, put it, "SBG taught our salespeople how to ask the right questions to steer customers our way. SBG was the 'glue' that attached our field to our factory."

Moving on to the next case study, when I worked with SilverStream Software, I learned that the sales teams in the Western Region were working incredibly long hours every week in order to make plan. I'd like to share with you what Barbara Wehrie, the company's Director of Sales for that region, had to say after implementing our sales messaging program. It's a long quote but worth repeating here, "Prior to Michael's efforts the typical first sales appointment was a technical education on the features and functions of SilverStream's main product. Most meetings lasted three to four hours, involved the use of more than 120 PowerPoint slides, and required the participation of both a sales engineer and a sales rep. After a few brainstorming sessions with Michael, the regional team was able to quickly define and reorganize the sales material into three key reasons why the prospect should buy from SilverStream. For example, one of the value propositions we identified was that SilverStream enabled applications to be built two to three times faster than our competitors' offerings. All the related product features were then identified and organized to support this point — all succinctly captured in a single one-page document. We were also able to shorten our slide presentation to 40 slides and our initial sales appointment to two hours or less, without the need for a sales engineer. If that visit generated a qualified prospect, then the SE was sent onsite to provide a technical demonstration that would validate the initial presentation's key value propositions.

"The impact of these changes was immediate. The first time the new sales strategy was used, we closed a $100K sale to a Fortune 500 company in less than 60 days, and sales in the region overall increased around 35 percent. Equally as important, by eliminating the need for a four-legged sales call, the cost of sales was reduced, the sales teams had more time to pursue more opportunities, and we improved conversion ratios in the sales funnel." End quote.

Here's one more case study example for you. A financial software company I worked with, A3 Solutions, was in a classic David-versus-Goliath struggle. It was a smaller company but it had better technology than the larger companies it was competing with. The competition had been intensifying during the previous 12 months, and the company was finding it more and more challenging to hit its growth targets. I helped the company implement the Silver Bullet Sales Messaging System by organizing a cross-functional team and helping them determine the prospects' primary buying questions. We then did a workshop to develop compelling answers and conducted informational interviews with the company's prospects and customers to validate that the new messaging was persuasive. The result was that in just three months the company's sales pipeline had doubled in size and its close rate was up by 150 percent.

It's really rewarding to watch great sales messaging work as a "silver bullet" to improve results and revenues.

Wright

Thanks, Michael. These examples give me a much better appreciation for the power of the messaging strategy. So, what trends do you see currently in companies' marketing and sales programs? Any predictions for the future?

Cannon

Yes. Over the last few years companies focused primarily on cost containment. Now the focus is on growing revenues and marketshare, and gaining and sustaining competitive advantage. The impact of this change in corporate strategy, the big shift if you will, is that the marketing and sales functions are going to be run more like their manufacturing, finance, and operations department counterparts.

Here is what I see. Manufacturing has a set of best practices, for example, ISO and 6-Sigma, to improve the quality of the manufacturing process, such as higher yields and lower fallout. These processes are then supported by a host of software automation tools, such as MRP, ERP, etc. Similarly, Finance has a set of best practices, for example, FASB and Sarbanes-Oxley, to improve the quality of the financial statement. There is also a host of financial software automation tools to support and improve the effectiveness of these processes. But when you look at the sales and marketing departments, what do you see? You don't see the same process excellence and discipline. What's missing is a formalized set of best practices for improving the quality of how these departments generate revenue.

This is going to be the big change. The Board and the CEO are starting to push the sales and marketing departments to be more accountable, more consistent, more predictable! They want a high-quality revenue generation process. They want Sales and Marketing to be more aligned around this imperative to gain competitive advantage and to improve their stock price.

What this looks like for Sales goes way beyond sales training. Companies are documenting and aligning the customer's buying processes with their own sales processes. They are documenting the series of conversations or steps that need to occur in order to walk with a prospect through the buy/sell process. They are also aligning the appropriate messaging, collateral, and sales tools with the revenue-generation process. Then they're overlaying new sales automation tools that help them quickly share best practices and support, enforce, and track these processes.

It's a big shift. What's occurring is that the art of selling is being forced to work in the context of sales as a business process and it's the right thing to do!

Marketing is feeling this pressure, too. Marketing ROI and marketing automation are very strong right now. Marketing is figuring out how to justify its expenses and tie those expenses to bottom-line contributions. They are developing formal processes for demand generation, lead quality, and conversions. They are figuring out how to more efficiently create, produce, and manage more effective deliverables, meaning messaging, collateral, sales tools, and field training. For example, I mentioned earlier that one of our clients, Agilent Technologies, recently revised its competitive training program and found that 56 percent of the reps were able to close at least one additional deal in the quarter after the training, because of the quality of the new training. Like Sales, the art of marketing is also being required to work in the context of a business process. That's a big shift in the right direction!

Wright

You have certainly given us a lot of ideas to digest, Michael! What specifically do you offer companies that could help them make the concepts and practice of great sales messaging part of their sales and marketing DNA?

Cannon

First, there are many free resources on the Silver Bullet Group website, such as free articles, sales messaging examples, and audio interviews. I also invite readers to join the Silver Bullet Group e-mail list, which gives them a free newsletter and keeps them posted on upcoming radio talks and other events of interest. Visitors to the site will also find several self-study tools, such as on-demand audio programs, e-briefings, and a recommended reading list.

For companies that want to rapidly plug into the power of sales messaging, we offer onsite or virtual messaging audits and sales messaging workshops to help with a new product or service introduction or to help boost the sales of a lagging product.

Also available are programs that can be configured to serve a company's specific needs, whether it's improving field product training or competitive training, developing training programs to teach Marketing how to create and integrate great sales messaging into its new product launches, or improving demand generation. [Note: Silver Bullet Group contact information can be found at the end of this interview.]

Wright

Today, we've been interviewing Michael Cannon, founder of the Silver Bullet Group. Michael, thanks so much for walking us through your impressive sales messaging system and how companies are using it to improve the quality of their messaging. I'm sure there are plenty of marketing and sales executives out there who'd like to hear more.

Cannon

Thank YOU, David! I really appreciate the opportunity you've given me to help more people understand how they can use great sales messaging as a "silver bullet" to dramatically improve messaging quality and the effectiveness of all their sales and marketing investments. It's been great talking with you.

About the Author

MICHAEL G. CANNON is an internationally renowned sales and marketing effectiveness expert and author, most recently coauthoring with business guru Brian Tracy, the best-selling book, *Create the Business Breakthrough You Want* (Mission Publishing, 2004). An expert in working with B2B companies to increase marketshare, revenues, and profits, Michael has assisted hundreds of companies — as big as AT&T and as small as a one-person startup — to increase revenues up to 1,300%! Michael is Founder and CEO of the Silver Bullet Group and creator of the hugely successful Silver Bullet Sales Messaging System, a proven, proprietary methodology for dramatically improving the quality of B2B messaging. Michael has addressed numerous audiences around the world, including *Entrepreneur Magazine Sales and Marketing Radio Show*, the American Marketing Association, the Silicon Valley Product Management Association, and Vistage International. Michael lives in the San Francisco Bay Area with his wife, Nicolle, and their daughter, Ariana. When not helping companies boost their marketshare and revenue, Michael enjoys visits to the wine country, dining out, cooking, and camping in the Sierra Nevada.

Michael Cannon, CEO & Founder
Silver Bullet Group, Inc.
201 Vallecito Lane, Suite 100
Walnut Creek, California 94596
Phone: 925.930.9436
Fax: 925.476.0307
E-mail: mc@silverbulletgroup.com
Website: www.silverbulletgroup.com

Chapter 6

Greg Gudorf

David Wright (Wright)

Today we're talking with Greg Gudorf whose career stretches over thirty years of consumer electronics marketing, sales, and business development activities. As a teenager in a television and appliance store started by his grandfather in 1946, Greg learned the basics of serving the consumer and operating a small business firsthand. His career then progressed through a variety of retail, distribution, and manufacturing organizations including nearly ten years with Sony Electronics where he last served as Vice President of Television Marketing. Having traveled extensively, including internationally, Greg finds pleasure in meeting people of all cultures and exploring differences as well as similarities in varied approaches to life and business.

Greg, welcome to *Marketing Strategies*.

You're fond of reminding marketers to "fish where the fish are." What drives your thinking with that saying?

Greg Gudorf (Gudorf)

Well, one thing above all others is certain in the world of marketing—no matter how good your product or how strong your promotional offer, if you fail to get in front of the customer, success will forever elude you. In other words, if you don't fish where the fish are, your opportunities for success will be limited beyond the accidental, occasional lucky catch. After all, marketing is really about making sure you're in the right location with the right target in mind (you need to know exactly what sort of fish you're looking for) and the right bait presented in the best possible light for that target. When that happens, marketing is as fun as fishing and far more profitable.

Wright

So, tell us how you came to connect fishing and marketing in this way.

Gudorf

As a youngster, I enjoyed fishing about as much as any kid. Fond memories of fishing off a floating river dock on summer weekends compete only with early morning memories of the hot, fresh doughnuts we'd pick up on the way to the river. My dad and us kids enjoyed those outings and caught our share of fish. Later on, as my own boys were growing up, I initially had a hard time repeating the experience for them in the various lakes around our then Southern California home.

My wife would laugh and the boys couldn't grasp what all the fuss was about, as we went from spot to spot failing to catch any reasonable numbers of fish. Eventually, I wised up and went to the little neighborhood pond around the corner and set about catching and releasing four- to eight-inch little sunfish about as fast as the kids could get their poles in the water. You see, I'd finally gone right to where the fish were and my kids and I had a barrel of fun.

The lesson of that pond is a lesson for all of us marketers to heed: fishing where the fish are is far more rewarding than fishing where they're not! You likely learned this lesson very early in life anyway when as a child you were faced with a school fundraising task. Where did you go first? You went to parents, neighbors, and family of course—they were your logical first fishing places.

To exaggerate the point, you would not have taken out an advertisement in the Wall Street Journal to meet your school fundraising task because that's not where your fish were to be found. Such an advertisement might have generated a response or two and might have even been award-winning in its creative approach—agencies love to win awards. However, your personal, direct marketing appeal to your best customers (friends and family) was the best marketing return available and that's where you instinctively knew to concentrate your efforts.

It's really no different in the business world. Small business owners often comment that their best business-generating advertisement is their ad in the local Yellow Pages. Their efforts at newspaper advertising often produce hit or miss results but their Yellow Pages ad consistently delivers a steady stream of prospects to their business. What's going on?

Are the Yellow Pages that much better of a marketing vehicle than the local newspaper? Well, not necessarily. The key is that prospects using the Yellow Pages are very focused on finding what they're looking for there. In other words, they are "hungry fish" looking for what you offer. The Yellow Pages work so well for so many businesses because it ends up being the right location, with the right target customers (self-selected targets are always best) who are hungrily looking for what you offer.

Of course, the viability or draw of your advertisement in the Yellow Pages will have a lot to do with how many of those hungry fish are attracted to and take your bait versus your competition's bait. But compared to the more generic local newspaper, a good advertisement in the Yellow Pages is a great example of fishing where the fish are. (More about the importance of the right "bait" later.)

By the way, the same location-plus-target-customer mindset can be used to improve the value of your local newspaper advertisements. It's not a fluke that so many of the car dealer advertisements are grouped together in the same section of the daily paper. Car-buying fish everywhere have learned that when they're hungry for a new car, they can head to that section of the paper and have their fill.

And while the car advertisements are an easy example, most local newspapers can work with you to determine the best section of the paper, the best day of the week, and even the best neighborhood route for you to place your advertisement in to raise the odds that you'll be fishing where the fish are most numerous and open to your specific offering.

As a marketer, it's wise to always ask if all the available tools are being fully used to serve your needs by helping you locate the best place to go fishing.

Wright

So how about an example from your career of fishing where the fish are?

Gudorf

Many years ago, when I worked for General Instrument and the satellite television industry was driven by consumers willing to install a big, seven- to ten-foot dish in their backyard, a good example of this approach at work unfolded as follows: Faced with trying to cost effectively find customers for our satellite dishes and knowing that mass market advertising tools such as national newspapers and prime time television were out of the realm of fiscal possibility, we chose instead to carefully define what sort of fish we were looking for and then make sure that we fished explicitly where those fish were most likely to be found.

The first order of business then was to determine the parameters of what we thought our prospects—our fish—to be. We decided we needed to find prospects who lived in non-metropolitan areas of the country (they needed room for that big dish!). We further decided we could improve our odds if we focused on markets where the local cable provider had either an absolute minimum number of channels available or what channels they offered were at a relatively high monthly cost. In other words, we wanted prospects who were likely to have the physical room for the satellite dish and yet were being underserved by the cable operators who were the competition at the time. If we could find those fish and then present our offer of hundreds of channels from the satellites in the sky, we reasoned it would be quite attractive for them and result in very cost effective sales for us.

So with our target fish clearly in mind, we set out to divide all of the U.S. postal zip codes into metropolitan and non-metropolitan markets. Specifically we were sorting for "C" and "D" county rural zip code locations. With that subset in hand, we then secured a list of zip codes from a cable television industry association that recapped zip code by zip code how many channels of television were offered and for how much in monthly fees. Combining the two lists gave us a stack ranked listing of zip codes across the United States where little television choice at a high cost was the rule and therefore potentially home to ideal candidates for the product we were offering.

If our hypothesis was correct, the stack ranked list would lead us to rich fishing locations for the prospects we desired. Given our list, we then began direct marketing solicitation using the relatively inexpensive, zip code based, bulk mailing services of the U.S. Postal Service to test and tune our offering (bait). The hypothesis panned out as consumers really did want more television choices at a lower cost (go figure!) and thus we had several years of good fishing and sold lots of satellite television equipment for ourselves and our dealers.

Wright

In the United States, there are some 40,000 zip codes, 12,000 school districts, and nearly 3,000 counties—to name just a few data types. How do you sort through it all to find the fish you want?

Gudorf

In the real world of fishing, over 80 percent of fish species swim together in schools. They do this for familiarity, safety, and convenience reasons, or so I'm told. Likewise, we humans tend to "school" together. While we live in a diverse, melting pot of a world, our homes tend to be located in and around people whose values and tastes are more alike than different from ours on many fronts. About now you're likely thinking, "Wait a minute, that can't be true. I have some really weird neighbors!" The reality is that nine out of ten times though, you and your neighbors are more alike than not. Your homes are of similar style and value, your incomes are not so day-night different, and even the cars you drive tend to be similar. Such a clustering of similar demographic traits within a particular geography (geo-demographic clustering) can be a powerful tool for marketers who want to fish where the fish are located.

Spend some time perusing the U.S. government's census site (www.census.gov) and the wealth of information waiting to be tapped will underscore this natural schooling tendency. As mentioned, income is a common "schooling" trait in that there are always differences in income levels between zip code areas even within the same community. Use the census site to take a look at the Rancho Santa Fe zip code of 92067 and compare it to the nearby Rancho Penasquitos zip code of 92129 to see how widely they differ.

While these two San Diego, California, communities are less than ten miles apart, the household income in Rancho Santa Fe in 1999 dollars was nearly $200,000 (one of the highest in the United States), while the incomes in Rancho Penasquitos did not quite reach $80,000. Further, the median value of a home was just over one million dollars in one zip code and just under three hundred thousand dollars in the other. You can guess which home value matched which income and therefore which zip code! This is important "schooling" information to know as a marketer.

The point is that the folks within each of these zip codes are more alike in terms of income and house value than they are different among their neighbors. Each zip code is a "school of fish" with a level of shared traits and general buying habits. The U.S. Census site is chock full of demographic data that when evaluated can become a powerful geo-demographic fish-finder in the hands of a motivated marketer.

If thinking about the rich potential of such a fish-finder gets your marketing wheels spinning, check out the tools and data available from various companies such as Claritas (www.claritas.com). The folks at Claritas can combine U.S. Census data with lots of other data sources to enable a powerful view into the "school" so you'll know if the specific fish you're looking for are likely to be in a particular geography. Their tools can also be used to determine the bait that's best used to land that fish.

Wright

Oh yes, you mentioned you'd address the issue of "bait." Do you have an example?

Gudorf

Sure; a project I worked on while at Sony Electronics several years ago used Claritas' zip code driven tools to help us determine a profile of our best customers for a certain product. Among other things, we learned that our best customers for this particular product were:

- 100 percent more likely than the general population to read Rolling Stone magazine
- 66 percent more likely to have played golf twenty plus times in a year
- 30 percent more likely to have purchased a new domestic auto

Armed with that knowledge, could you create a marketing message and campaign that might successfully reach such a prospect? You bet. A reader of

Rolling Stone who plays a lot of golf and has recently bought a new domestic automobile is a very specific type of fish! And that's exactly what we did by focusing our message and communications on marketing and advertising tools we knew would deliver a story that the prospect would be highly pre-disposed to react well to.

What's more, given other data sources Claritas delivered, it was even possible to zoom into what brand and model of domestic auto as well as what brand of golf balls such a prospect might use. By the way, thanks to the data from all the store shopping "clubs," so many of us and our neighbors use to get the occasional discount on our purchases, it's even possible to predict with good accuracy what brand of toothpaste our Rolling Stone-reading, golf-playing, new-auto-driving prospect might use every morning

Wright

Is all that as much work as it sounds to be?

Gudorf

Of course, it's much easier for a business owner to say, "I just want to buy an advertisement and get some customers." Accordingly, there are lots of people who will help you spend your advertising money. Beware! There is no shortage of opportunity to simply cast away your marketing budget.

Back in the real fishing world, I've been known to cast a line at a nearby lake without a thought as to the bait I'm using; sometimes I don't even use bait! My wife laughs (again) as she knows I've got little chance of catching anything with such an approach. I don't mind, however, because sometimes I'm just sitting by the lake lazily turning a reel and drawing a line through the water. Truth be told, I want the relaxing activity of the casting and reeling but not the bother of catching a fish! That's okay for a lazy evening at the lake, but is that any way to run your business's marketing campaign? Of course not! Unfortunately, many folks take a similar approach in their marketing efforts and, as happens all too often when no fish are caught, they blame everything except the fact that the wrong bait or no bait is being used—assuming they're even casting about in the right location.

If, however, you arm yourself with an in-depth knowledge of the fish you're hunting for and then use tools such as the U.S. Census and Claritas segmentation tools to fish where the fish are using the bait they are most likely to respond to, then your return on investment will be much higher and your marketing efforts will become the fun, profitable, results-focused machine you want.

Wright

How can you determine the best bait without lots and lots of trial and error?

Gudorf

There truly is no substitute for real world, real prospect-to-customer testing to hone and refine your message. However, an easy step you can always take is to ask yourself what it is that you want your marketing efforts to deliver for you.

Imagine for a minute that you're a small business owner looking over a new marketing brochure you've just had created to promote your services. It has your business card at the top, a big picture of you or your building and words like "best," "caring," etc. You beam with pride at the platitudes of goodness staring back at you. However, in evaluating your new brochure, the question you should first ask is, "What do I want the brochure to deliver for me?"

If you want it to drive business with new clients and have them react by contacting you for specific next steps, then a brochure proclaiming motherhood and apple pie platitudes will miss the mark by a fairly wide margin. In fact, Mom and your ego may like seeing your picture and reading a platitude-filled piece about your business, but real-world prospects will likely ignore it the way fish ignore bad bait. And yes, your agency may have designed a brochure (or advertisement) that looks nice, normal, and very typical of a brochure that any of a thousand other small businesses might use. This does not automatically mean it meets the basics of a good marketing piece. Neither will such a piece deliver for you if the true nuggets of information written into the brochure are buried so that they hardly see the light of day with potential clients.

The basic task of any marketing piece is to:

1. capture the attention of the target market

2. provide some information gathering and decision-making elements for consideration

3. make it easy for a prospect to take the next step

Thinking of the fishing world, the action, and appeal of the bait catches the attention of the fish while the presentation of the bait and the way it delivers the hook is what allows you to reel in your catch.

Back in the marketing world, these three steps need to serve the same function. There is a book titled Monopolize Your Marketplace by Richard Harshaw that has good examples of this approach to marketing. Harshaw explains the classic marketing equation as follows:

• Interrupt: Get qualified prospects to pay attention to your marketing. Accomplished by identifying and hitting your prospects' hot buttons.

• Engage: Give prospects the promise that information is forthcoming that will facilitate their decision-making process.

• Educate: Identify the important and relevant issues prospects need to be aware of and then demonstrate how you stack up against those issues, thus building a case for your business.

• Offer: Give prospects a low-risk way to take the next step in the buying process. Put more information in their hands and allow them to feel in total control of the decision.

So, evaluate that shiny new brochure from this new perspective. Look for how it conforms to the classic interrupt, engage, educate, and offer equation. Not so well? Let's probe a little deeper to see how it stacks up against the equation in detail.

First, look at the cover. It is what needs to do the job of interrupting and engaging. This part of the brochure needs to get the prospect to pick up the piece and open it. It needs to be the equivalent of fishing with the right bait for what you wish to catch. Is that picture of you or your building interrupting and engaging? Will it make a prospect pick it up? I don't think my grinning face on a brochure will do that but maybe yours will.

What about that business card? A typical small business brochure fondly features the company's business card in a prominent location as if it were a headline. Just placing it there does not make it a headline. It is not a "hot button" and besides having your address "in" the business card and at the bottom of the front cover, as is typical, is dedicating a lot of precious space to the part of the brochure that simply needs to get qualified prospects to pay attention.

Wright

So, if your business card is not a hot button, what hot buttons should you use on the front cover to appeal to your prospects?

Gudorf

The initial presentation of the bait may excite the fish but the scent and movement are the hot buttons that beget the nibbling prior to the bite. How do you find hot buttons? One good way is to ask yourself under what circumstances are prospects inclined to think about what you offer? Or another: what is important to prospects when they are trying to buy the services you offer? There must be dozens of potential hot buttons ranging from frightening to nurturing that you can draw upon for your marketing needs. If you're stuck, ask your customers what they were thinking before they decided to become customers.

A better headline than your business card might be "Three Problems with XYZ . . ." followed by a subhead that might say, "How Our Business Can Overcome Them All." Another example would be "Thinking about XYZ? Don't Have the Foggiest Idea Where to Begin?" Then add a subhead that would say, "Three Things You Need to Know about How to . . ." will give the benefits you're promising.

Once your cover gets the prospect to pick up and open the brochure, you've got a fish nibbling and your fish bobber will be bouncing along. Inside the brochure you have lots of space to provide direct, real-world examples that deliver on the promised "Three things you must know . . ." sub-head from the cover. This is your space to educate the prospect by identifying important and relevant issues for them. Make the inside spread really work for you by sharing in story form—as if you were talking to a friend—real examples of real people and how having your help enabled them to protect, serve, enjoy, or otherwise counter/address the hot buttons your cover raises.

Don't be afraid of lots of text but do worry about the font size being too small. I've become particularly aware of that little problem with age and the demographic trends say many more of us are in the same category these days. Also, watch out for lists of information in an attempt to cover everything as opposed to delivering information as a story in a way that specific prospects can best relate to and learn from. The primary job of this section is educating your prospects as to what you offer.

And don't forget to make sure the inside spread boldly promotes your "offer." You've got a great offer, right? Your offer is what enables the next step you want your prospect to take. Perhaps it is to "attend a free seminar" or "schedule a free consultation" or if you're a fish—to bite their way onto the hook! Don't let your good offer get literally buried in the text so that if your prospect is simply scanning, they will scan right by the offer and thus not take advantage of it.

By the way, creative agencies often grumble when you push back on their ideas with these marketing 101 basics, however, the results of following the formula speak for themselves every time. And yes, you should test, test, and test some more in order to tune and maximize your marketing efforts. However, you can improve almost any marketing effort in advance by asking yourself the simple questions noted above and then running the work through the wringer of the equation as detailed.

Wright

All of these ideas seem appropriate for direct mail, printed newspaper, and Yellow Pages forms of advertising but do they apply in an online world?

Gudorf

Actually, the same principles are just as powerful and even easier to apply in the online world! Spend some time in the world of Google AdWords (www.adwords.google.com) and the related WordTracker (www.wordtracker.com) and you're sure to learn lots to profit from. In the online world, the challenge is still the same—you need to find where the fish are that you want to reach.

The bad news is that in the online world you don't have the real world's geographic segmentation to assist you in your hunt. The better news is that you have highly traceable behavioral elements that can help with locating prospects far more accurately than in the real world.

As an example, if you want to find out what fishing fans find when they go looking online for a new fishing rod, you only have to type "fishing rod" into a Web search box to instantly see what prospects see. If you type "fishing rod" into Google you'll get about 150,000 results, all talking about fishing rods in one way or another. Now the good news is that you're fishing in a big school when you see that many results. Before you panic at how you can possibly stand out among all of those results, dig a little deeper.

First, did you notice a selection of links at the top of the results page? Those are paid advertisements for which a business owner has decided to buy an impression and place his or her offer in front of all the people who search for a fishing rod on Google. You can do the same thing by using Google's AdWords service, which we'll discuss more in a minute. So, how do you decide on the right keyword to "buy" via AdWords?

Well, recognize that Google alone spawns more than ninety million searches from online users every single day just within the United States. Luckily, services such as WordTracker allow you to better understand what it is that people are searching for across multiple search engines and how many prospects are doing the searching. Unlike the Yellow Pages, WordTracker can tell you how many times a particular phrase has been searched and predict how often it will be searched every twenty-four hours.

For instance, if you check "fishing rod" at WordTracker, the first thing you'll see is that lots more prospects search for the plural—fishing rods than they do the singular term, fishing rod. In fact, based on an analysis of millions of keyword searches over the past ninety days, WordTracker predicts that nineteen people will search for "fishing rod" every twenty-four hours while the plural form will be searched for sixty-six times in the same twenty-four-hour period on just one major search engine alone. Subscribers to WordTracker can see similar predictions for lots of different search engines.

Secondly, WordTracker can tell you how many other Web sites and businesses are competing for that term via listing and purchasing such keywords so searchers might be offered their link as a search result. In the "fishing rod" example, there are over one million competitors. That alone isn't a problem; it merely means the cost of buying that word in AdWords will be more expensive because there will be a lot of competition to "own" it. You see, the online keyword market works on a supply-and-demand basis with high demand words commanding top dollars to be positioned first where prospects are most likely to click upon it and thus visit the seller's site. It often pays to be a bit more selective. For instance, if you dig a little deeper in WordTracker, you'll find that the keywords "Fenwick fly fishing rods" has only sixty-five competitors. Of course, they also predict only one fish will visit every twenty-four hours!

You can easily learn how all of this works and even get a sense of what keywords (bait) the fish are searching for by using these sites to test various words and combinations. AdWords is Google's main source of revenue—it is a big business. Are you using it? You simply choose the keywords you wish to trigger your advertisement and then establish how much you're willing to pay for the placement. The rest just happens. Of course, if you've chosen your keywords poorly you may or may not realize that traffic. And even if you generate the traffic, if your destination doesn't deliver on the expectation you've created with the keyword advertisement, then your conversion to sale rate will quickly skew the wrong way, driving your return on investment negative.

Remember that the online world is not just about Google and search results either. Check out what Jeep, the manufacturer of the original all-American, go-anywhere sport utility vehicle, is doing in the Web 2.0 space. You'll find a Jeep Flickr (photo) feed, a Jeep YouTube (video) feed, and Jeep pages already built out on both the MySpace and Facebook communities. Jeep's online efforts are yet more great examples of taking advantage of the behavioral "schooling" of fish in the online world. Relating with your prospect in such a way that they become part of your spread-the-word marketing community is just good business. Such completeness of the marketing circle is tough to pull off anywhere outside the online world.

You can dive into this part of the online world by learning to participate in the myriad of blogs, networks, and services on the Web with the goal of making your business's participation a source of relevant information—in other words, good bait—for the schools of fish swimming online.

So the online world is a great place to go fishing and the tools are evolving rapidly to really leverage the tracking power of the connected world for both the benefit of the marketer and the customer.

Wright

Any final comments for us?

Gudorf

Well, my niece and aspiring writer, Jordan Hallbauer (thank you, Jordan!), put it into a poem for me to summarize the approach quite nicely:

Were I to fish,
and do it right,
I'd not fish in a place
where the fish swim light.
No, I'd find a place
where the schools are many,
And cast the bait,
though not just any.
It'd be a bait
for the special fish
that my stomach wants
upon my dish.
Then I'd wait for the catch
and reel it in
again and again;
my technique always wins,
for when you fish where the fish are
And use the right bait
It's more work now, but later

You'll have more fish on your plate.

So, go ahead. Go fishing. Whether it's online or offline, just make sure to fish where the fish are with a specific kind of fish in mind and the best bait you can develop. If you do, your marketing will shine and your business will thank you for it.

About the Author

GREG GUDORF currently serves as Chief Operating Officer of Digeo, Inc., a developer of digital video recorder products for the cable and consumer electronics industries based in Seattle, Washington. Greg often speaks at industry events, holds multiple patents in the consumer electronics arena, and has been published in industry magazines and periodicals. He is a co-author of the book Speaking of Success in conjunction with Stephen Covey and Brian Tracy. Greg is also a member of the National Speakers Association and the American Marketing Association.

Greg Gudorf
E-mail: greg@gudorf.net
Blog: www.gudorfgroup.com
www.gudorf.net

Chapter 7

Richard Weylman

David Wright (Wright)

Today we are talking with Richard Weylman, CSP, CPAE. He is an overcomer. An orphan at the age of six, Richard lived in nineteen foster homes. Richard's perseverance and success, despite a seemingly stacked deck, inspire people to overcome their circumstances.

He is a master marketer and an entrepreneur. He worked in tough markets, with unique products, from his earliest days selling cookware, to helping build an award-winning Rolls Royce dealership. He is the former head of sales for the *Robb Report*, an internationally known magazine for the affluent lifestyle. As president of his own consulting firm, Richard works with clients to help them grow their business with affluent and high net worth people.

He is the author of *Opening Closed Doors, Keys to Reaching Hard to Reach People*, published by McGraw Hill. Forbes calls this book brilliant. As an authority on marketing to affluent and high net worth people, particularly executives and entrepreneurs, he has authored several content-rich sales, marketing and management programs that have been adopted by some of the world's largest companies. These interactive programs are available in several formats including audio and video as well as through his online university; in addition, programs can also be commissioned to suit organizations' unique needs.

He is not only a consultant, but also a member of the National Speakers Association. Richard has achieved the highest earned designation of Certified Speaking Professional (CSP), has been inducted into its Speaker Hall of Fame and, most importantly, has received The Council of Peers Award of Excellence (CPAE). He joins fewer than one hundred fifty speakers so honored including Art Linkletter, the late Norman Vincent Peel, Zig Ziglar, Ken Blanchard, Harvey McKay, and others.

Richard, welcome to *Marketing Strategies*.

Richard Weylman (Weylman)

Thank you David.

Wright

I'm interested in one of your articles entitled, "Growing Your Business with the Affluent and Wealthy." How do you gain access to the right people in the right way at the right time?

Weylman

To gain access, it is vital to have a plan; not just a marketing plan, or a work plan, or a good idea plan, or even a merchandizing plan. The plan that I'm speaking of to gain access, is a plan based upon what the affluent, or if you will, the financially successful think.

Years ago when I was working in the Rolls Royce business, I had a good client I met with. I told him what I would like to do to market to more people like him. I said, "I think I would like to do this and I would like to do that." I was articulating my marketing plan. He put his hand up after about three or four minutes and said, "Richard, let me just tell you this – wealthy people don't care what you think. We are not even remotely interested in what you think. What we are interested in is, first, can you understand what and how we think and, secondly, can you communicate from our point of view?"

That was a watershed moment for me. I then began to recognize that, too often, our plans are based specifically on what we think. Yet once one understands the affluent perspective and their point of view, you can then create a plan that can truly put you in front of the right people in the right way at the right time. A plan that is focused on their point of view has three components:

- The first part is the process you will use. How are you going to focus your efforts and resources? How are you going to segment these individuals? What type of visibility are you going to achieve with them? What are the specific methodologies you will use? What will be the process you will use to become part of their network? How will you be able to service and support these people? What will be your service culture? What will be your support culture?

- The second part of the plan is the message you are going to deliver. In other words, a lot of people think that you have to be different, but to be different is polarizing. First I have to compare you with something to be different. Of course, the larger objective is not to be *different* from everyone else, but to be *distinct* from everyone else, to be set apart. If you talk to affluent people, they will tell you that they look for organizations and individuals that can distinguish themselves. What will be your message? How will it resonate with them? How will they respond to it? Will it be in their words, their voice and their perspective? What approach will you use? How will it be distinct from all others?

- The third component of the plan is how will you humanize and personalize the process so that you can connect to them? It is critically important to ask yourself, "How are we going to communicate at all different levels with prospects and clients so that they can see that we are focused on them, that we are not just customizing, but personalizing our process? How are we humanizing the approach and experience so that they can connect to the fact that we are focused on them and not just on our product?" In other words, in the end, to gain access to the right people in the right way at the right time, one must focus as a marketer focused on people, not as a merchandizer focused on product.

Wright

How do you market to the people and not to their wealth to set yourself apart from the competition?

Weylman

Fundamentally, you must understand what the affluent want from you irrespective from the product or service that you offer.

What do the affluent want? The first thing they want is someone who is truly interested, i.e., passionate about doing business with them, and understanding about their goals, aspirations, complexities, and their issues. Essentially they want you to be focused on them, engaged with them, interested in their way of life, interested in their issues, with a knowledge of the things that motivate them.

The second thing that the affluent want is consistency of communication. Affluent people want you to stay connected, not *ad nauseum*, but they want to know you are there for them.

At the same time, they do not want you to call just to "touch base." What is the value they are going to receive if you are simply calling to touch base? There is no value there for most people. Most affluent people are very busy and the idea of you calling to touch base not only indicates that you really have nothing of value to bring to them but they feel, many of them entrepreneurs and executives, that you are simply wasting their time. On the other hand, if you call to discuss issues, address topics, give them insight, further brief them, keep them up to speed, keep them on pace or to let them know the latest issue, that kind of messaging resonates because they see value in it.

It is essential that you have a communication plan for affluent clients. Ask them how often they wish to be contacted. What are the best ways for your messages to be communicated? The key to all of this is: what is the messaging – does it have value to them? It really needs to be a balance of the following: some of it needs to be relationship building, while other times, on calls and messaging, it needs to be an opportunity to inform, educate, and brief them on topics of interest. Remember, out of sight is not out of mind, out of sight is on your way out of their business circle.

The third thing that the affluent want today is someone who is willing to listen. Listening is so rare today in most sales and marketing arenas that the financially successful complain openly about the fact no one "listens to them." We show up at client and prospect meetings with "our" agenda, ready to talk about "our" agenda, fully prepared, so when we sit down with an affluent constituent, "we" immediately launch into the agenda that we want to cover today. The way to demonstrate to people that you have a willingness to listen and hear what is on their mind is to simply stop at the very beginning of the meeting, and tell them that you have an agenda you would like to cover today, but before you get into the agenda you have one question for them: "What are three things you would like to get out of this meeting today?" Prospects and clients alike are thrilled their input is solicited openly! By setting that table it gives them permission to talk about the things that are important to them. It demonstrates clearly that you have a willingness to listen to what is important to them.

Fourth, and finally here, of the many things the financially successful want, they are really looking for direction and guidance from the individual with whom they are doing business. They want to know that with every decision they are making they really have someone who is a sounding board for them, helping them to find, get on, and stay on the right track to a good decision.

Whether they are buying a high end stereo, a home, a high end automobile, or investment products, people want direction and guidance. Individuals and organizations are meeting with you to discover what you know. Thus, when you meet with people it is important that you engage with them and find out what is important to them. To spend the first ten or fifteen minutes talking about you, your capability and ability wastes their time. You would never have been given an appointment with a financially successful individual unless they thought you had capability and ability.

To execute these ideas effectively, you have to be curious, you have to become a student of the financially successful and you have to plug in and get to know them. Read everything you can read, observe them and connect to them so that you begin to understand what it is that the financially successful people in your community, in your market, want and are seeking.

Wright

Do you have a method or technique designed to build relationships with the affluent that create loyalty and foster long-term commitments?

Weylman

First I believe one of the great myths perpetrated on American business and businesses around the world is that if we have satisfied clients we're in terrific shape. In the affluent marketplace, a "satisfied" client is loyalty neutral. A satisfied client says things like, "Sure, I'm pretty happy there. I'm pretty happy with their products and service. They are nice people and they do a pretty good job. I'm not unhappy, I'm pretty satisfied. But, if you hear of something else let me know, I am always open to something better or at least a new idea."

Thus, once you recognize that a satisfied client is loyalty neutral, then you have to realize that to be effective creating loyalty and fostering long-term commitment, it begins with a focus on people, not on product, and it continues through the experience they have with you. Many products and services that are being marketed everyday are a commodity in the marketplace. The only answer to commoditization is personalization and humanization of process. As an example look at Starbucks. Starbucks delivers a product and service that is a commodity. They provide a product and service that you can purchase anywhere for $1.00 to $2.00 a cup, and yet they are delivering it for $5.00 to $7.00 a cup. The question is, why are people continuing to go to Starbucks for their product and service and, secondly, why are they so loyal and committed to Starbucks as a brand? It is because of the experience they receive at Starbucks: the warmth, the ambiance, the language, the service, the freshness, and the personalization. The total personalization is that you order exactly what you want. They don't just customize it, they personally produce it for you right there while you wait. As a result, they have transformed their customers and now these individuals no longer care how much it costs to go to Starbucks. They are absolutely delighted clients of Starbucks who will stand in line to buy and receive Starbucks coffee. Why? Because of their experience and the fact that Starbucks believes that if you sell a product you should get service. Most people in this country think, "Well, the thing that sets us apart is we service what we sell." In our country service is *expected* on any product that we buy. To suggest that service is something that distinguishes you or creates delighted clients is to live in naiveté. The only thing that changes a satisfied client into a delighted client is to give them an experience that transforms them. A satisfied client needs a unique experience to be elevated to a delighted client.

So to build relationships that create loyalty and long-term commitment, here is a series of questions that you should consider:

- How is everyone greeted in the office or in your store? If I walk into the average office and I'm not a client, many people walk by in the hallway and never even speak to me, even if I am walking with another one of their colleagues. At the Ritz Carlton, every employee, from management to housekeeping, is taught to stand and to turn to the guest and greet each one. They want to create a sense of an elevated, unique experience.

- Do you know what your clients' and prospects' preferences are? Do you know your clients' preferences in beverages, what they would drink if they come to the office? Do they want bottled water – still or sparkling? Do they want regular coffee or decaffeinated? Are you elevating the experience? Are you serving it in china cups and saucers and crystal, or do you think that it is too much work, and not giving them an elevated experience? If you stay at a Ritz Carlton or Four Seasons hotel, or go to a high-end retailer like Neiman Marcus, Bergdorf Goodman, or Saks and you ask for a beverage, they always bring it to you in a crystal glass, and many of them bring your drink in china cups and saucers.

It is a matter of creating a unique experience. Clients and prospects are looking to be treated in a way that elevates their thinking about you and allows them to distinguish you from all others. It's often the little things that matter most. Do you have a modifiable service plan that, if I purchase something from you, you can service me in a way I want to be serviced? Do you have a 24-hour, 365-day emergency telephone number? You might say that you gave them your cell phone number, but that is not the same positioning as giving them your cell phone number and identifying it as their 24-hour, 365-day emergency phone number.

Building relationships and creating loyalty is not just limited to how clients are treated or cared for – it is the portfolio of memories you create that matters as well. Many think that sending people tickets to sporting events is a good idea; but, what matters the most is the elevated experience of being personally engaged with them at the event. To build a portfolio of memories, invite them to events that are central to what they are passionate about. Give your clients and prospects events that they can't buy, but experiences that they will remember for a lifetime and connect to you. This is what builds loyalty and long-term commitment. They are no longer just buying a product or service, but rather, they have such wonderful experiences it transforms their thinking about you. You become part of their network!

Wright

Would you give our readers some insight as to how the affluent define value and make purchasing decisions?

Weylman

First, most decisions revolve around emotional security. Thus, you have to create a safe place for affluent people to discuss issues of importance and their concerns. It may be they want to ask you questions about a product, a service, or a process. Or it may be they want to talk about some type of anxiety in their life which is the precursor or obstacle to a purchase decision. In the end, you have to create a safe place for them to talk about their fear, uncertainty and their doubt, or as I call it "FUD." We have to be able to demonstrate to them that we care enough about them that they can feel safe discussing issues of importance and interest to them even if they seem trivial to you. They place extraordinary value on getting themselves heard and understood.

One of the key things to remember about the affluent and particularly the wealthy, the further up the economic ladder you go the harder it is to relate to other individuals. The harder it is to connect to individuals who are in a less affluent place. Many see it as aloofness or arrogance. Sometimes it is, but much more often they are just guarded. There is a great deal of concern about their economic security; they protect that by keeping a wall around their emotions which can limit their ability to connect to people. By creating this safe place for affluent people, they understand and observe that you are genuine about them and they receive great value from this because you represent a sounding board. They want a sounding board, somebody with whom they can relate, somebody with whom they can connect, someone who will energize their thoughts, someone who will engage them on a completely different level to help them to be able to sort through, work through, and make the right decision. That becomes part of their value assessment of you.

Which brings us to the second part of how people define value and make purchasing decisions. You must realize that how you are perceived, talked about in the marketplace, and the message you promote, (i.e.: your unique value proposition), is what sets you apart. Your unique value proposition is a statement of who you are. By articulating what you do for others, they catch that it's not about you, it's about what you do for others! Thus, it positions you in the marketplace. All of your promotion emanates from this unique value proposition. It is your way of helping people understand what it is that you can do for them. So your unique value proposition is not a focus on what you do such as having great service or years of experience, or a unique process, or a unique product, but a unique value proposition is how it meets and how it addresses issues important to them. A unique value proposition says, "We are able to help you achieve a desired objective." Whether that objective is future vision, reducing their anxiety, or living a better life, in the end your unique value proposition has to say "Here is what we are able to help you to achieve."

By speaking their language they immediately understand value and know that you can define value in their language, which reduces their skepticism and ultimately boosts confidence in them that you "get it".

Wright

You wrote a great book, *Opening Closed Doors, Keys to Reach Hard to Reach People*. Was there ever a time when you had trouble reaching the hard to reach and how did you solve the problem?

Weylman

My very first sales job was selling cookware door to door. When I started out, my manager told me that "everybody buys our cookware." I was excited – I thought selling was mostly a delivery service. I ran out and started going door to door and after about eight or nine days I wasn't getting into anyone's house. It was awful. I went back to my manager and told him this was not working. He wanted to know what I was doing. I told him that I had tried everything. Now, when they opened the door I was even putting my foot in the door, that way they couldn't slam the door on me. He wanted to know if I was crazy. He told me that he just heard Bill Gove, a speaker (who I was privileged to meet many years later), and he wanted me to practice what Bill said to do. Bill said, "Don't put your foot in the door, put your head in the door; that way, when they slam the door you can keep talking!" Wow!

That made me realize that sales keep you in business, but only marketing keeps you in sales. I began to realize that if I was going to be effective not only did I have to be good at sales I had to understand marketing, not just product merchandizing or marketing, but true experiential marketing – marketing that builds knowledge of the prospect and thus a relationship that is based on a terrific experience.

The first thing I did was go to the library. I did research on neighborhood groups and found the best demographics I could (that was before the Internet). Then I went to work. I began to sell cookware. I was very successful at it because I was in the right neighborhoods with the right message with the right people. I marketed my services with warm introductions, neighbor to neighbor, created dinner parties and cooked for clients' friends, friends who were my prospects, and focused on delivering a great experience!

When I went into the industrial laundry business, renting doorway rugs and mops, I targeted retail stores with high traffic in strip malls. There was a lot of dirt tracked in right out of the parking lot which was just six to eight feet away. I mopped and swept lots of floors to demonstrate how much was being tracked in. I created an experience they could see. I kept those clients too by changing their mops and rugs more frequently in the winter so they could give their customers a better in-store experience.

Today, if you really want to be effective opening closed doors you should Google and research every single prospect. Capture what they do for a living, what they do for recreation, what their special interests are. By doing so, you have leverage and increased confidence. You can speak their language, connect with them, and build trust almost immediately by understanding where they went to school, what they are passionate about, what organizations they are involved with, how they are involved in the community, and what their level of interest is in a variety of things. All of these things come to bear by helping you open closed doors. It all goes back to the late Bill Gove's point years ago when he told that manager, "Don't put your foot in the door, put your head in the door; that way when they slam the door you can keep talking!" Little did he know then that truly you *can* use your head before you go in the door!

Finding out about your prospects long before you show up, in today's business world, requires that you realize the sale begins long before the salesperson shows up.

Wright

You said that most sales professionals are so busy running the business that they don't invest the time or effort to grow the business. What can be done to change that pattern?

Weylman

The first thing is to understand your points of leverage. Most people don't think about leverage, they just think about working hard, working smart and other sayings that are thrown around by people. There are really three components of leverage:

- The people around you
- The resources available to you
- The efforts that you are putting forth

The challenge we face today is most people are not leveraging the people around them or their resources or efforts.

If you look at each of those and you begin to understand the leverage you have in each of those components, then you begin to recognize that you can spend more time growing the business and less time running it.

Let's examine first the people around you – your support staff. Do they have proper job descriptions? How much time are they wasting every day on jobs they are not qualified to do? How many things are they doing over? In my office the theme is "If you don't have time to do it right, when are you going to have time to do it over?" Having to do it over just drags the life out of them and what happens is people are overwhelmed having to repeat things and tasks. Another question to ask yourself about the people who are working with or around you is: have you invested in systems to increase productivity? How many dollars every year are you investing in software, middleware, and hardware to be able to increase productivity? Leverage comes when your team can work faster, more effectively, and have the personal recognition that they are moving forward.

Finally, on this leverage component, when is the last retreat you had with your entire staff to solicit their input on how you could delegate more and streamline all processes? Why not find out how they can relieve you so that you can get free of the day-to-day work to focus on growth? What are some of the ideas they have? What are some of the ideas that you could imitate or they could initiate to help you to get free so you are able to move forward in the process?

Perhaps you should hire a marketing intern to be able to help you or maybe an administrative intern. Maybe they could suggest a couple of people. Maybe if students get out of school early, they could work parttime to get your firm on their resume. The reality is that people around you have good insight in how things could be streamlined. How are you leveraging that insight from their practical day-to-day activities to get you free to grow?

The second leverage component is the resources available to you. Have you identified these resources? Maybe the product, service, or process that you sell perhaps has marketing dollars or co-op programs available; are you aware of them and are you using them? Are you using the intern programs that some companies already have in place to execute your best projects? Are there educational resources available to teach you how to market and sell your services most effectively? Have you engaged in a study group of about four or five peers who are in the same industry as you to get a sense of what the best practices are, what is really working, how you can benchmark your progress, and how you can get yourself free to grow the business?

How about the vendors who are calling on you, who are selling to your business? They see other businesses like yours. Do they have some insight about how other people are growing and how they are getting themselves free? How they are getting themselves in a position to expand their business? Lunch with a vendor marketing to you and your clients is a meal well spent.

The third component to leveraging is managing the efforts you are putting forth. In other words assess what your time is worth. If your time is worth $250 an hour, how much time are you spending on $10, $15 and $20 an hour jobs? Most people who are not growing their businesses are spending most of their time at $10 to $20 hour jobs and then suggesting that they don't have the capital to invest in growth. If you were to hire someone to do the $10 - $20 hour job it would free you to go out and grow your business; a business where your time is worth many multiples of $10 or $20 per hour.

To be able to execute effectively, from my experience, you have to flee the need to own every job, and pursue the role of leadership in your organization.

The business will only grow based on your ability and willingness to invest in services that free you. If you are not willing to invest in services, you won't be able to grow your business. You will spend the second half of your career running the business that you've grown in the first half.

So, in summary, to grow your business you have to understand your three leverage points: the people, the resources and the effort you are making.

Wright

What is a great way to execute new business ideas effectively?

Weylman

Create a series of 90-day plans for your business. The advantage of 90-day plans is that you can almost see ninety days ahead. In thirty days you can certainly see sixty days. It brings a lot of energy, excitement, and a sense of accomplishment to yourself and all your people. So to begin, when you have a list of things you want to accomplish, whether it be changes you want to make to leverage yourself so that you can get free to go back to growing the business, or new ideas to improve your personal life, develop a 90-day plan. First, list what you want to accomplish specifically. *Dwell in possibility* is what Emily Dickenson said and she was exactly right. Make a list of what you want to accomplish – very specific things such as hire an intern or update software.

Second, define the steps you are going to take. Adults like steps. What steps are you going to take to accomplish these specific tasks?

Third, identify the obstacles and be real and specific. Obstacle: "I'm going to have a hard time letting go." Obstacle: "I'm going to have a hard time getting people to agree to this." Write down the obstacles.

Fourth, assign dates and times to get this done. The value in this is you get focused, and with focus you get vision. Most importantly, with a 90-day plan, you have an opportunity to have a clear and direct path to get things accomplished. I will tell you from our own experience corporately, it helps me to identify what is not working long before it is really not working. It helps me to modify more quickly to leverage the people around me, the resources available to me and the efforts that we are putting forth.

Wright

Would you use a real life example to demonstrate how the readers can expand their business profitability?

Weylman

Here is a story from an e-mail I just received from a client we have been working with for eighteen months. The person is in the financial services business and is the head of a wealth management team that is part of a much larger global organization. Their team is not in a wealthy state but they are in a state where there are of course wealthy people. They are not in a large metroplex, but they have a rather substantial financial management practice they have built throughout the region.

The first thing we did was to sit down with them and help them to understand the mindset of the wealthy in their area. We did some research to discover the mindset of the wealthy in the area that they were going to be targeting.

Secondly, we assessed the culture of their organization. How were clients treated when they visited: the offer of a beverage, the greeting, the ambiance? We created service protocol – the who, the what, the why, the when. We talked about how the service calls were going to be communicated effectively and how we were going to be able to repeatedly deliver excellent and consistent communication.

We had them investigate and determine how well they knew their clients, their values, their charitable giving, their cultural activities, their ethnic connections, their religiosity, and their family connections as well.

The third thing we did was sit down and create a unique value proposition that clearly spoke to the constituent target, wealthy people, that they were trying to reach. In this case, it was families with over fifty million dollars in investable assets in their geographic region – a very narrow and difficult market to crack, because you know every single one of those families already has a financial firm working closely with them. We were going to have to dislodge their existing provider and move them to this particular group.

The fourth thing we did was create a master plan to modify the things we had assessed together that had to change in their team, their communication, their culture, and their mindset. Then we created a series of 90-day plans to execute. Every ninety days we revised and continued to execute the process, the procedure and the discipline to move people along. Our objective long-term was to move each change to be made into their business rituals and culture.

As a result of consistent integration of these changes and very hard work by this team, I'm happy to report that in eighteen months they were able to acquire eight new fifty million dollar plus household families. They were moved from firms where they were satisfied to my client's firm. My client's firm now has nine additional fifty million dollar plus households in various stages of moving who should all be moved within the next nine months. This means they will have increased their money under management nearly one billion dollars in a two-year period by following the outline we've articulated here.

Wright

In all of your experience, what have you found to be the key reason that people cannot seem to overcome the obstacles preventing them from developing their business to its true potential?

Weylman

There are many reasons. However, from my experience here are the three most prominent:

- There is a lack of vision. – There is a wonderful proverb that says "people without vision perish." I think people resign themselves to living an average life. The other side of that is people with vision prosper. Unfortunately, most of us are taught to be realistic. Don Hudson, a fellow CPAE and professional speaker, said once that "people set realistic goals, but what they ought to be setting is realistic time frames." I thought about that and I realized he was exactly right. I was an orphan. My mother died when I was five and my dad died when I was six. If I would have been realistic I certainly would not have the opportunities that I have today. I think what we need to do is have big goals, a big vision, and then set realistic time frames. This focus on realistic thinking leads to a lack of vision and prevents people from overcoming obstacles so they settle for the average or status quo.

- The second reason people get caught by the obstacles is people become victims of circumstances. The way they think, the way they operate, is heavily influenced by others and the circumstances in which they find themselves. There is a lot of victimology in society today. People say that they can't or didn't do more with their life because they had a tough up-bringing or didn't get the right education and so on. The reality is that being a victim is unfortunate. Letting it rule your life is a choice – a choice usually reinforced by hanging around the wrong people; people who also are making that same choice and/or have a negative general outlook. About every six months I make a list of people I no longer want to be around. I know that if I associate with negative people who see themselves as perpetual victims, they are going to throw cold water on every idea I think of, conceive of, or want to execute. They are going to try to get me to be a victim of my circumstances. I don't want to be a *victim* of my circumstances; I want to be a *victor* over the circumstances.

- Finally, insurmountable obstacles for many result because there is not a clear cogent process to execute. They have no plan, no process or discipline. Instead of commitment and declaration, it is just the "Someday" approach. "Someday I'm going to be successful." "Someday I'm going to be wealthy."

"Someday I'm going to own a new car." "Someday we are going to buy a house." "Someday I'll get married." "Someday we'll have children." To facilitate and move past "someday", be proactive! In business, hire a contractor, create a team, meet with your staff, get together with a peer group, and find a way to begin a plan, a process, and discipline to move forward. The longer you stand around saying "someday I'll", someday will never come. Many years ago Dennis Waitley wrote books on this topic and I never forgot what he said about "someday I'll". As Dennis said, many people go to the end of their lives with "wish-a, could-a, might-a, had-a", because they took the "someday I'll" approach. To facilitate in your personal life find a mentor or coach. Find somebody you can partner with. Associate with more positive people. Find people who have a forward view as opposed to a past view. As long as the past is an option, the future is very unclear.

Instead of finding an excuse, find a way. I can tell you that when I first started in business, I had no money. I went to a nursing home and found a woman who could type. In those days typewriters were the big thing. I paid her by the letter because I couldn't afford to hire her. She typed the letters I hand-wrote. Be relentless, make a commitment and declare your plan.

Wright

Today we've been talking with C. Richard Weylman, CSP, CPAE. As an authority on marketing to the affluent and high net worth people, particularly executives and entrepreneurs, he has authored several content-rich sales, marketing and management programs that have been adopted by some of the world's largest companies.

About the Author

An orphan at the age of six, Richard lived in nineteen foster homes. Richard's perseverance and success, despite a seemingly stacked deck, inspire people to overcome their circumstances.

Master Marketer and Entrepreneur – Richard worked in tough markets and with unique products – from his earliest days selling cookware to helping build an award-winning Rolls Royce dealership to being head of sales for the *Robb Report*, an internationally known magazine for the affluent lifestyle. As president of his own consulting firm, Richard works with clients to help them grow their business with affluent and high net worth people.

Author – Richard is the author of *Opening Closed Doors, Keys to Reaching Hard to Reach People*, published by McGraw Hill. *Forbes* calls this book brilliant. As an authority on marketing to affluent and high net worth people, particularly executives and entrepreneurs, he has authored several content-rich sales, marketing and management programs that have been adopted by some of the world's largest companies. These interactive programs are available in several formats including audio and video as well as through his online university; in addition, programs can also be commissioned to suit organizations' unique needs.

Professional Speaker CPAE Hall of Fame – As a member of the National Speakers Association, Richard has achieved the highest earned designation of Certified Speaking Professional (CSP), has received the Council of Peers Award of Excellence (CPAE) and has been inducted into its Speaker Hall of Fame – joining fewer than one hundred fifty speakers so honored including Art Linkletter, the late Norman Vincent Peel, Zig Ziglar, Ken Blanchard, Harvey McKay, and others.

C. Richard Weylman, CPAE, CSP
Consultant, Speaker, and Author
Richard Weylman, Inc.
P.O. Box 436
Boca Grande, FL 33921
Phone: 941 828 3600
Fax: 941 828 3604
E-mail: office@richardweylman.com
www.richardweylman.com

Chapter 8

Robert Bly

David E. Wright (Wright)

I'd like to welcome Mr. Robert Bly. Bob is the author of more than 50 books, including *The Complete Idiot's Guide to Direct Marketing,* published by Alpha Books and *A Copywriter's Hand Book,* published by Henry Holding Company. His articles have appeared in numerous publications such as *DM News, Writer's Digest, Amtrak Express, Cosmopolitan, Inside Direct Mail*, and one of my favorites, *Bits and Pieces for Sales People.* Bob has presented marketing, sales, and writing seminars for such groups as the United States Army, Independent Laboratory Distributaries Association, American Institute for Chemical Engineers, and the American Marketing Association. He also taught business to business copywriting and technical writing at New York University. Prior to becoming an independent copywriter and consultant, Bob was advertising manager for Koch Engineering, a manufacturer of process equipment. He's also worked as a marketing communications writer for Westinghouse Defense. Bob, welcome to *Marketing Strategies!*

Mr. Robert Bly (Bly)

Thanks, and thanks for having me.

Wright

When I first began to look at your career and the scope of your works, I was amazed at how prolific you've been. You wear many hats and seem to be an expert in many fields. How would you describe yourself? Can you give our readers a brief overview of your life's journey?

Bly

I don't think of myself as versatile or a renaissance person. I really only do basically one thing. I may do a couple of others, but I describe myself, when people ask, as a freelance copywriter. Now sometimes people who are not in marketing don't know what that means. So I say to them then, "You know how you get home and you have all that junk mail? I like that direct mail." That's how I answer it. So then they understand it. And my journey is odd. I'll give this short version and you can find the full story in some of my books. I started out young being interested in science. I wanted to become a scientist. I majored in chemistry in college. And then I realized I wasn't particularly good at it and I switched to chemical engineering because I thought that would be a better job. When you're a college senior in engineering, companies come on campus and interview you. And when I talked with one of the interviewers, the person said, "You seem awfully interested in writing. Our company needs technical writers and your background would be ideal." So Westinghouse hired me as a marketing writer for their Aerospace and Defense Division in Baltimore. And that's how I got started in copywriting and marketing.

Wright

I'd like to start with a question about one of your more high profile books, Bob. You authored *The Idiot's Guide to Direct Marketing* for Alpha Books. My guess is that if you ask 10 business owners how they felt about direct marketing or what they thought direct marketing was, you'd probably get 10 different answers. How do you describe direct marketing? And can you give us examples of direct marketing techniques that you've found to be effective?

Bly

The easiest way to describe direct marketing without using jargon or sounding like a college textbook is that direct marketing is a kind of marketing where the reader has to respond in some way. Either they request a free catalog, a sample or a demo, or they order the product. There is a direct response. That compares with what we call general advertising or Madison Avenue advertising which doesn't ask for an immediate response, but rather tends to build and create an image for a product or build what we call brand awareness. The example would be an auto commercial, a commercial let's say for an auto dealer that says to come in Saturday and Sunday, test drive a car, and get a free bottle of champagne. That's direct response. You're asked to take an immediate action versus when you see a Coca Cola commercial. They don't expect you to call a toll free number and order some Coca Cola or run out then, but they're thinking you'll think about Coca Cola next time you go to the supermarket or the next time you go to a diner. And that's really the difference.

Wright

Do companies use both methods at one time?

Bly

There are some companies that are pretty much strictly just direct marketers. There are some companies that are just strictly what we would call image or brand or general advertising. And then there are a lot of companies, probably the majority, that combine both.

Wright

Is there one size or type of business that should use direct marketing campaigns while others should not?

Bly

I don't think there's a size or type of business that should or shouldn't use direct marketing. I tend to think that if you have a small or even a medium sized business, you know you're not a Fortune 500 company, that direct marketing is really almost the only marketing you can afford because you don't have a million dollar budget like Coke or Pepsi. You're never going to build that big brand awareness that they can do by running a commercial eight thousand times. You would go bankrupt. You would go out of business. So if you're a small business, you need to see an immediate positive ROI, return on investment, from your advertising and marketing and really only direct marketing gives you that. General advertising, image advertising does not.

Wright

So what else can you tell us about direct marketing that might help our readers understand its effectiveness?

Bly

To do direct marketing, you have to have what we call in the business, and most of your readers will be familiar with this, you have to have what's called an offer. An offer is basically what the person gets when they respond to your marketing combined with what they have to do to get it. So an offer might be, for example, mail back the enclosed reply card and you'll get a free inventor's kit that tells you how to make money with your invention. That's an offer. And without that offer, direct marketing is going to get minimal response. With that offer, it will get very large response. So you always have to have an offer, and it has to be perceived as having high value. And it either needs to be free or risk free. In other words, you offer can be, "Send me a check and I'll send you a product," but it has to be risk free. You have to say, "You just use it for 30 days and if you don't like it, return it within a month and we'll send your money back."

Wright

You're considered one of the best copywriters in the country. Many of the consultant services you offer business revolve around the written word. Where does this fit into the larger issue of marketing for small and large businesses?

Bly

Businesses…all businesses close their sales with words. Some businesses are marketing driven and some are selling driven. With some products and some businesses, the person who will close the sale is a sales person, and so using these words, he will sit and talk to a prospect or customer one on one to convince him to buy the product. In other businesses that are marketing driven, there either isn't a salesman or the salesman plays just a partial role. So, it's your marketing, whether it's a website, catalog (if you're selling fashions or whatever), the words, whether they're on a computer screen or printed on a piece of paper, close the sale. And for the businesses that are direct marketing driven as opposed to sales driven, the way you construct those messages, the writing, the copywriting is tremendously important. The more business depends on direct marketing to make the sale, the more important words are. Some businesses don't. Some businesses, a few of them, are built on cronyism, whoever knows this other person gets the job. And in that case copywriting and marketing aren't that important.

Wright

I've done a fair share of copywriting myself over the years, and I've also created marketing campaigns for my companies. I've always thought a great marketing campaign begins with a great idea. Do you find that many elaborate and expensive marketing campaigns seem to have been built on an ineffective concept or idea?

Bly

Yes. In fact, this is the number one marketing mistake. Whether the copy is poorly written or well written, whether the piece is nicely designed or shoddily designed, is very much secondary in importance to the idea, as you call it. There's an old quote from Samuel Johnson, who said, "Advertising is built on a big promise." Or his exact quote was, "Promise large promises, the soul of an advertisement." So it's the idea of what you promise. How does that product meet a need or a want or fill a requirement of the buyer is much more important than any advertising in the way it's executed. There's an old saying, which I think is largely true, that if you have a great idea, offer a product that people will really want, especially a targeted group of people, you'll probably be successful even if your advertising isn't great. It would be better if it was great because you would be more successful, but that can work. However, if you have a lousy idea, something that's you know or no idea, no matter how eloquently you word it or how cleverly or brightly you promote it or package it, it's not going to sell. And I do think that's true.

Wright

What kind of process do you take your clients through to help them reassess their marketing plans? And do you find many businesses are resistant to change?

Bly

Basically, if people are interested in this, and I'll answer the question for here, but if people are interested, I think that's so important a process that actually on my website (www.bly.com) I have a button on the home page. It's a choice of buttons, and one of them says "methodology." I make the process very visible to my potential clients whether they want copywriting or consulting or what have you. And that actually is part of my methodology. I think people want to know how you will work or how you will solve their problems. In many situations it is useful and beneficial to let them know that. My step in doing a marketing consultation is to gather as much information as I can about two subjects—the product, but also the audience, the potential customers. I've got articles on the website that outline that process in detail. One of the other common problems, you said you yourself, you need a big idea or it doesn't work. The other one is that people, marketing consultants, contractors are lazy. They offer quick solutions without gathering the information first. And almost always the solution or the answer comes out of the existing material. You're not creating anything. You're just presenting it in a different way. So you have a lot of front end research to do if you're helping other people. Even if you are doing your own product, you may know a lot about your product, but it's amazing how a lot of people don't really understand their audiences or their markets and what they want, and they don't bother to do that. If you don't do that, you increase the odds of failure tremendously.

Then you need to define what is the specific marketing problem that you want to solve. Do you want to generate more leads? For example, someone will come to me and they'll say, "Well, we need to increase sales. They're lousy." But that's too vague and I question them. And they say to me, "If we get a prospect in front of a sales person, we close 80% of the time." So closing is not their problem. But their problem is getting a sale person in front of a prospect. They couldn't get that meeting. So then the problem became how do we get more inquiries from prospects who are willing to sit down with a sales person and spend time with them so we can quote them. And once you define that, then there's a limited repertoire in the world of tools and techniques that you can use. And based on experience, knowledge, and testing you can find out which will work for that particular situation, implement them, measure the results, and then refine them and fine tune them. And that's what you have to do.

Wright

You're also considered an expert in the business to business marketing. Can you give us an example of this kind of marketing? And tell us what makes the most effective business to business marketing.

Bly

Let me give you one example of what works, and it happens to be a subject I'm actually writing a book on now. Business prospects generally are information seekers in a way many consumers are not. For example, if I see an ad for Burger King, I don't need to know how the hamburgers are made, how Burger King runs its operations. I just want a good tasting hamburger. But if a business buyer is buying a product or service, they want to understand because whether they do their job well or not depends on how effectively they buy products and services and manage their vendors. For example, if you sell a network firewall, your customer wants to know how the firewalls work. How do I know I'm choosing the right one, right?

Wright

Right.

Bly

One kind of marketing that works very well is—there's a term for it, I don't know if I made it up or someone else did—edu-marketing which means educational marketing. You can win the buyers confidence and generate a high degree of interest by offering to educate them about the problem your product solves or the methodology of your product. For example, if you're selling firewalls, you might offer what's known in the software industry as a white paper, which is a free report called, *How to Measure Your ROI* (return on investment) *from Installing a Firewall*. Because if I am an IT manager and I go to management and say I want to spend $40,000.00 on a firewall, the owner of my company doesn't know anything about IT, doesn't care. He says, "Well, what's that, how's that going to pay off. What am I going to get for that $40,000.00?" So this white paper will show me how I can demonstrate that if he spends $40,000.00, we'll make that back in the first month by preventing internet fraud or preserving network band width or whatever the wave a firewall generates all our life. That kind of marketing works especially well in business to business.

Wright

I was perusing your titles on amazon.com, and I came across your book, *Fool Proof Marketing, 15 Winning Methods for Selling Any Product or Service in Any Economy*. This really caught my eye because I love it when experts break down their ideas into manageable bits. Can you touch on one or two of your favorite methods from this book?

Bly

My original title for this, which the publisher changed to *Fool Proof Marketing*, was *Recession Proof Marketing*. So the book, as you could tell from the subtitle, is really about selling products or services in a recession or slow economy. The book does have 15 specific techniques for doing that. I'll give you one of them. One is to offer your products or services in smaller packages. In other words, in a good economy, let's say you're a consulting firm and your normal consultation is $10,000.00. You'll find that when the economy slows down, maybe your potential clients who normally spent that without a problem, may be hesitant to spend that much money, and so therefore they're not coming to you at all. If you decide to offer a more scaled down version and you call it *The Quick Start Consultation* and that's only $2500.00, a lot of the people who now are not buying you service because of the $10,000 price point will start working with you again and buying the $2500.00 service. You'll make money on that, but also once they start with that, they'll want to continue and will eventually spend the whole 10 grand anyway and go on to the full service. That's one strategy. Another one that's more general, but really almost more powerful, is during a recession or slow economy the service provider who's going to win more business is the one who's going to be most flexible and accommodating. You know that a lot of companies, when they have more business than they can handle, they shift into a little bit of a prima donna mode. We've all called architects who happen to be busy and said, "Well, I can't squeeze you in until the year 2012." There's a funny Tom Hanks movie called *The Money Pit* where he wants to hire a plumber and the plumber doesn't even look at the job. He says, "Give me $5,000.00." Tom Hanks gives him the money. He goes, "When will you be back?" He says, "I'll let you know," and he drives off. During a recession, you can't do that because suddenly the work is dried up and now it's a buyer's market. So you have to be much more flexible, accommodating, and willing to do what the buyer wants in order to get his business. That's another strategy.

Wright

Before we wrap up, Bob, I'd like to shift gears to public relations. I've always viewed PR as a vital component of a great marketing plan. How do you feel about the value of public relations for businesses and what advice would you give our readers related to PR as a part of their overall marketing strategy?

Bly

Well, though I do direct mail and direct marketing, and I say it is the most effective method, direct marketing is expensive. PR is great because it can get great results, fantastic large results, and it's relatively inexpensive. It's something, in fact, you can do a lot of it yourself. Now, I actually have co-authored a book on this topic called, *Public Relations for Dummies*. I wrote it with Eric Yaverbaum, who has a PR agency in New York. I'm a big fan of this. In the book we discuss all the PR strategies, but here's what I would say. The easiest way to do this is to identify the publications (and I'm leaving out radio and TV and the internet) that your prospects read, whether it's the local town paper or if you sell mechanical equipment, maybe it's *Chemical Engineering Magazine*, and write, not ghost write, write. Call the editor and offer to write an article related to your product for the magazine. In other words, if you sell mixing gear for chemical plants, write an article for *Chemical Engineering Magazine* on 10 ways to size a mixer. That will be going back to that edu-marketing we talked about. You can write that article and it might end up being two pages in that magazine, you don't pay for those two pages. You're bio with your company's phone number and website URL runs with that article, and if you bought those pages as ads, they'd probably cost you $10,000.00. And they're yours just for the worth of writing. In fact, some magazines will even give you a little honorarium so maybe you'd get 50, 100, 200 bucks out of the deal. That's the way. That's the place to start with public relations. You don't need to read my book to find out how to do that. If you go to www.bly.com and look on the articles page, you'll see an article there on public relations titled, *In Search of Ink* that tells you exactly how to get editors at pub magazines and trade journals to have you write articles for them and run your articles.

Wright

What about direct mail, Bob? Many of my colleagues have totally moved away from direct mail in favor of internet marketing. What do you think about these two methods of marketing?

Bly

There are a couple of basic answers. Let me give one. You can't predict it. That is just the way it is. Some businesses work very well with print(direct mail), and the internet doesn't work so well for them. Others work great on the internet and it's just a waste for them to do direct mail. And there are a lot of others who are very successful at combining the two methods. The thing, of course, that is in favor of internet marketing is the hugely lower cost. But here's the problem. In direct mail, I can go to a list broker, rent a mailing list of people who are strangers. They don't know me. They don't know my company. I can write a letter and send it to them and they will send me money to buy my product or they'll reply at least to ask about buying my product if I'm generating leads instead of sales. This does not work in internet marketing. If you rent a list from a list broker, an internet list or what they call an e-list and you try to sell people who do not know you a product, you're response will usually be 99 times out of 100 abysmal. You'll lose money. So you say, "How are all these people making all this money in internet marketing?" What you'll notice is that all of the people who make good money in internet marketing, big companies, but a lot of small entrepreneurs and operators have large in-house lists. They have built up a list of 5,000 or 10,000, or 20,000, or 50,000 names of people whose e-mail addresses they own and they can mail to them any time. Usually they did this by offering a free online newsletter. Like on my website, I have an online newsletter that goes out once a month. It's called a direct response letter. I have over 70,000 subscribers. So if I send to that list, I can send an offer to that listing.

I have a new report. It's $20.00 and you can download it by going here. You know the response rate will be high because these people are interested in what I do because they hear from me every month. There are three reason it works to e-mail to your house list. Number one, they're interested in you. They know you and they want more of what you do. Number two, they will accept an e-mail from you versus if they get an e-mail with a from line from somebody they don't know. They won't read it. And number three, mailing to that e-list is basically free. You know I can e-mail a message to 70,000 people at almost no cost. So internet marketing works for people who have built up a large house list, usually easing subscribers into it.

Wright

If you had just five minutes to spend with a CEO of a small or mid- sized company, what would you tell him or her about marketing that might help them the most?

Bly

Here is the other common mistake. We talked about not having the big idea, which was your comment. The other is not having an offer.

Wright

Right.

Bly

Here's the other mistake. CEOs of small and mid size companies will call me and ask for advice. If I say direct mail, for example, they'll say, "Oh, direct mail doesn't work." I'll say, "Really? How do you know that?" Then they'll say, "Well, we did a mailing and it didn't work." That's really dumb.

What typically happens is the small company will write or produce a very poorly executed post card, sales letter or sales mailing. They send it out, and of course, it doesn't work because there's no offer. There's no big idea. There's no value. And then they conclude that the entire category of direct mail doesn't work. The big companies don't do this. For example, you've seen commercials for Blue

Blocker sun glasses. So Joseph Sugarman runs that company. He's one of the great mail order marketers of all time. I listened to a lecture he gave. He said that when they did magazine ads for Blue Block they would sell; they never did just one ad. They would do three or four versions of the ad minimum, and usually 10 versions. Sometimes they would do 10 versions and nine of them would bomb. But the one of the 10 versions would make so much money that it would pay for all the other nine, and then they knew that they could keep running at a profit. So if he just ran one of those other nine ads, he would conclude that space advertising doesn't work. He would have stopped. What you should do in direct marketing, if you're small, is look at the big direct marketers like Joseph Sugarman and do what they do. The one thing they do all the time that small marketers don't do, but should, they test. They test two or three headlines, three or four mailing lists, two or three offers. And by testing in small manageable quantities, you can start to find out the combination of copy, art, design, format, list, media that make money, that have a positive ROI. As soon as you find that, it's like a money machine that can make you money. If you get a direct mailing that generates 200 sales for every $100.00 of cost in the mailing, that's like having a machine where every time you pull the lever it turns a dollar into two dollars. And that's what you need to do. You need to test on a small basis.

Wright

Goodness. What a great conversation. I wish I had met you years ago and taken all these notes. My business would be a lot further along. Today we have been talking with Bob Bly, respected copywriter, marketing consultant, and author. Bob, thank you so much for taking this time with me this morning and I really, really do appreciate it.

Bly

It's been an absolute pleasure. Thank you.

About the Author

ROBERT BLY has written copy for over 100 clients including, Network Solutions, ITT Fluid Technology, Medical Economics, Intuit, Business & Legal Reports, and Brooklyn Union Gas. Awards include a Gold Echo from the Direct Marketing Association, an IMMY from the Information Industry Association, two Southstar Awards, an American Corporate Identity Award of Excellence, and the Standard of Excellence award from the Web Marketing Association.

Bob is the author of more than 50 books including, The Complete Idiot's Guide To Direct Marketing (Alpha Books) and The Copywriter's Handbook (Henry Holt & Co.). His articles have appeared in numerous publications such as DM News, Writer's Digest, Amtrak Express, Cosmopolitan, Inside Direct Mail, and Bits & Pieces for Salespeople.

Bob has presented marketing, sales, and writing seminars for such groups as the U.S. Army, Independent Laboratory Distributors Association, American Institute of Chemical Engineers, and the American Marketing Association. He also taught business-to-business copywriting and technical writing at New York University.

Bob has appeared as a guest on dozens of TV and radio shows including, MoneyTalk 1350, The Advertising Show, Bernard Meltzer, Bill Bresnan, CNBC, Winning in Business, The Small Business Advocate and CBS Hard Copy. He has been featured in major media ranging from the LA Times and Nation's Business to the New York Post and the National Enquirer.

Robert Bly
Copywriter
22 East Quackenbush Avenue, 3rd Floor
Dumont, New Jersey 07628
Phone: 201.385.1220
Fax: 201.385.1138

Chapter 9

Andrew Finkelstein

David Wright (Wright)

Today we're talking with Andrew Finkelstein, founder of The Beauty Resource. He is an entrepreneur, author, speaker, and professional coach. He publishes *The Finkelstein Report*, the professional beauty industry's leading salon and spa management guide. As a business executive he directed over 750 salons and has both created and worked with some of the most highly recognized professional beauty salons and day spas in the world.

Andrew is a much sought-after marketing coach, mentor, and business advisor to owners and managers of professional salons and day spas who want to attract more clients and generate more profits. He helps his clients identify their business strategies and achieve results through his products, presentations, and programs.

Andrew, welcome to *Marketing Strategies!*

Andrew Finkelstein (Finkelstein)

Thank you, David, I'm glad to be here.

Wright

How in the world did you ever get involved in the beauty business?

Finkelstein

I guess you could say that the beauty business is in my blood. You see I grew up in a very large extended family. We got together on holidays and virtually every weekend—for me life was family, and family was life. So family was a very important part of my life.

It just so happens that my dad's family was involved in the beauty business. My dad and his two brothers owned a company called Glemby. Although not every member of his family worked in the business, it was a large enough business with different branches, including an international division, so if a family member wanted to join the business he or she could.

Our family was very well known in the business all the way back to the 1920s when my grandfather had bought out the Glemby brothers who were the original owners. Through the years my grandfather and his sons build a reputation of being a family who stayed together through thick and thin.

I'd worked summers in the business and then I went to college, but truthfully, I never really intended to get involved in the business. After college I went to work for Federated Department Stores (now known as Macy's) in their executive training program. This training program was the on-the-job equivalent of getting an MBA in the retail business.

One day as I was working I got a call from one of my cousins who were at the time the executive vice president of the family business.

"Hey, Andrew," he said, "come on down to our office and let's have lunch and have a conversation because we could really use you."

Those were sweet words to my ear. What person doesn't like hearing something like that? I really felt terrific about that. Here was an opportunity where I could be entrepreneurial and build something of value for myself and my family, and work with the people I loved. After a couple of conversations I decided to do it.

So I went to work in the business and started out as a receptionist in a beauty salon. I worked behind the desk learning the ins and outs of the service business.

I'm not a professional hair dresser or esthetician, but I've done nearly every other type of job in those types of work units. Eventually I ran a large group of salons for the company, with about five thousand people in the division.

Since I had a good feeling for fashion and I had a good sense of the numbers, I also ran the marketing department—what we called the Image Department. It was a combination of public relations, training, and development for managers and technical staff as well as advertising and promotion.

I have to say, it was great working with the family, and I spent seventeen years there. Then one of my uncles died, and his family wanted to get out of the business. The only way they could do that was to have the family sell the business, and the sale of the business took over a year. Sometimes things like that bring out the worst in people, and it got so bad during that year that the family blew apart. As that old saying goes, "The operation was a success" (we managed to sell the business), "but the patient died." So what happened was that this really great business ended up killing what I really loved, which was family. As a result of that sale, which was the defining moment in my professional life, I decided to dedicate myself to showing other people in the beauty business how to use marketing to build their businesses successfully. That's how I got into the business.

Wright

As familiar as you are with the salon and day spa market, what do you think are the keys to success?

Finkelstein

I'd say that it starts with leadership and the leader's vision. That is the critical key to success because without a vision you can basically forget about success. However, having said that, there's a lot more to it and I can break it down into eight key strategies.

The first key is to construct for the CEO or the manager a powerful vision, and usually it's a three- to five-year vision. I know in Japan they have hundred-year visions, but we're not in that culture—we're in the United States. And while vision might seem like an obvious thing, in our industry most salon and day spa owners do not take the time to sit down and create a vision that's going to pull their business forward. From this one step of creating vision, the strategy of how to build your salon or day spa or any other business emerges. And in addition, what comes out of this is the power that the owner can latch onto to build the business to whatever size business he or she wants to have.

The second key to success is taking the time and making the time to plan. Literally hundreds and thousands of day spa owners want to make more money, but they also want more freedom. They want more time to do the things they like to do, but they find out very quickly that they become a slave to the business—they are serving the business instead of the other way around. So you need to use tried and true planning techniques to create the space you need to build a large and sustainable business without driving yourself nuts.

The third key is that you have to get control of your finances, and along with that goes your pricing strategies. You've got to master the financial side of the business once and for all. Like many small business owners, they usually don't have this financial acumen under their belts, after all who are they? They are usually technicians and they've been cutting hair or doing facials and doing massage or doing nails and they've been doing it very well. They are usually working for someone else and they're probably the best technician in the shop, so fundamentally they know how to market themselves because they were usually the busy person at the business. They knew how to do that, but they didn't know how to run a business where the finances are the critical part of the business. They know the technical side of the business, but not necessarily how to build a business or anything about the administrative part of the business. And they certainly don't know the financial piece. So as salon or day spa owners they need to learn how to leverage the financial tools and financial resources available. They don't have to become accountants, and that's probably the last thing in the world they would want to learn how to do, but they need to know the basic financial skills and how the cash flow statements work. Once they understand that, they can hire a sharp accountant and have a good communication with that accountant. They can set up their compensation systems so that they work not just for the employees, but so the systems also work for the business. It's an absolute must to learn how to manage your cash flow, because cash is oxygen to your salon day spa—without that oxygen you know what happens to something.

The fourth key strategy is to build and lead a championship team. Let's face it—no one can do it alone. So if you want to build a great business without being a slave to it you have to build it through others.

Michael Gerber, author of *The E-Myth Revisited: Why Most Small Businesses Don't Work and What to Do About It,* wrote about working "on" your business and not just "in" it. Salon or day spa owners have got to adopt this powerful point of view and apply it to their businesses. Once they do, they'll learn how to identify the key positions in their business and how to find the people to fill those positions. Then they'll discover how to systematize the business in such as way that they can get on with doing what they have to do with a minimum of interference from the owner. The owner really has to learn to lead. It's very important. You'll see the thread that winds through these eight key strategies and that thread is systemization. This is because each of these strategies can be systematized. There is a system for how to construct a vision. There's a system for planning your time, as well as a system for financial controls and setting prices. There's a system for everything.

The next or fifth key strategy is creating a world-class customer service system and delivering what I call a "wow" experience. Let's talk about customer service and dig down a little deeper. The professional salon or day spa business, which is really a local business, has got to have a strong referral system. It's is still the number one way to filling the chairs and rooms. But to have a referral system you've got to have great customer service systems in place. Otherwise why would someone refer your business to another person, especially someone he or she cares for? Frankly, they wouldn't. So creating a world-class customer service business and delivering a "wow" experience is one of the eight key strategies.

The sixth key strategy is refining your ethical selling skills. But most folks in the salon or day spa business (or let's face it, in most businesses in general) say they hate selling. In this particular business—the beauty business—most people get into the business because they love people. So what's absolutely necessary is to create a system that helps you, the owner or manager, and your people, overcome any fear you may have when it comes to talking about your services or products. You also have to build a proper language to use to get your customers or clients to buy your products or services beyond what they say they come in for. There's both an art and a science to this. You have to master it. So devising a selling system and refining your selling skills are absolutely essential.

The seventh key strategy is developing a steady flow of new clients and helping the old ones purchase more by using low-cost marketing techniques. When I look at marketing it's really a straightforward process. Sure, I know there's a lot of mumbo-jumbo that people sometimes heap on the marketing pile. But marketing is straightforward. Having said that there's still a specific way of marketing, and if you don't follow this specific way, you'll put your salon or day spa behind the eight ball.

Salon and day spa owners know they have to market; but they really don't know how. So they end up throwing out a lot of money because they've latched onto ineffective and costly marketing techniques that are being tossed around the industry as gospel, such as the need to build an image. If the owner/manager learns some simple methods that work they'll be a lot better off. Plus they'll be surprised at how easy, pain-free, and fun these techniques can be. Why in the world should marketing be painful anyway? You've got to have a steady stream of new clients and you've got to learn how to use low-cost marketing to get them.

The last key strategy is maintaining a balance in your life between work, rest, and play. If we look at it, owning a salon or day spa is not just about the money. Sure, money's important. After all, everyone wants to be able to earn a living. You have to pay the bills and you want to go out to a nice restaurant now and then, take a vacation, and live a good life. You'll want to put those money pressures behind you—you know what I mean. So the critical thing here is you have to view the salon or day spa as a vehicle to bring you the kind of life that most people only talk about. And you'll make more money for sure when you put those strategies in place and follow them. But more important than that, you can actually have the work-play balance you dreamed of when you first started your own business.

So, David, those are the eight key strategies to salon/day spa business success.

Wright

What are the greatest challenges facing salons and day spas today?

Finkelstein

Today they face three main challenges. First they have to differentiate themselves in the marketplace. The day spa business has grown by leaps and bounds; people have seen that it is a good business to get into and everyone's jumped into it. So when the marketplace is crowded you have to stand for something and be different.

The second challenge is that they have to find and keep good people, and the third challenge is that they have to attract and keep good clients. And wrapped around that is the fact that they have to do those three things while keeping the cash flowing positively. If we take a look at what is happening in the entire U.S. spa industry, hair salons are only one component—the industry also includes independent spas. The gross for day spas was $9.7 billion in 2005, which was up from $7.0 billion in 2003 and that's huge.

And there's a component of the business that is growing particularly quickly, and it is day spas and hair salons in hotel and resorts. Five years ago only about 10 percent of U.S. hotels and resorts had spas, and now it's up to 25 percent, according to Spa Finders, an industry tracker. Those statistics are very significant, and it just further emphasizes the need for day spa and hair salon owners to differentiate their businesses in the marketplace. So that goes back to the challenge of what's facing them. If you're an independent salon or day spa owner (and I'm not really talking to hotel operators, although they certainly have a similar challenge of differentiating their business in the marketplace), how do you become the place to go in your community? How do you become "that place" clients think of first? Basically, salons and day spas are local businesses, and the way you position your salon or day spa is very different than positioning, for example, a hotel in Las Vegas. You don't have a captive audience like the big spas in Vegas do, so the question is how to capture your local audience. You do it through differentiation and you differentiate yourself through your marketing.

How do you find and keep good people? Salon and day spa owners and managers have two types of customers: internal and external customers. As large a challenge as it is to market to the consumer out there, owners and managers also have the challenge of marketing to the service provider. There are not only more choices out there for the consumer, but there are also more choices for the service provider who, in most instances, is a licensed operator. You need to become a beacon or place of choice for the top people in the profession to work, and you want to attract them. You have to do a good job of marketing to them.

Wright

How do you keep good clients and good workers?

Finkelstein

You build a business that provides the things that the clients want. You have to focus narrowly and niche down—study what they want and choose your market carefully. You have to become an expert at delivering the products and services. You have to build systems and structures within your business—training systems where employees can learn new techniques, management systems, financial systems, and support your internal business. Then you have to build a marketing system that's going to attract clients. These are mandatory today if you want to meet those challenges.

Wright

If you could give one piece of advice for *new* businesses, what would that be?

Finkelstein

It would be to have a marketing plan and to operate from that plan—a short, solid, executable plan. Most salons and day spas don't have a plan and didn't start with one, which is the reason that over half of them go out of business within the first five years. And next to the loss of a spouse or a loved one or the loss of a significant relationship, going out of business is absolutely devastating. It creates havoc, not just on the owner, but on the extended families of all the employees and all the people who have come to trust that particular business—it's a big thing. Most of these businesses didn't start out with a plan that they could use on a day-to-day level, and the importance of that is the one piece of advice that I have for anyone.

I'm not talking about an intricate, extensive financial plan. I'm talking about a one-page business plan/marketing plan, maybe two pages at most. One would be for the business, and the other for the marketing of the business.

When you're operating an independent hair salon and you've hired yourself, as you grow you owe it to everyone who comes to work with you to have a plan. Some view this plan as something that is just a financial thing that has to be taken to the bank or the Small Business Association to raise money for your business. While that can be the purpose of a plan, and is required to get money for a project, some people just do that and avoid putting together an operating plan which eventually causes them to fail rather than succeed.

Wright

If you could give one piece of advice for *established* businesses, what would that be?

Finkelstein

If you don't have a plan, build one immediately! Through the plan you'll create your vision, you'll create your mission, and you'll create your objectives, your strategies, and a list of actions that you have to take in order to reach your objectives. Through that process and the planning, you'll be able to see where you are and where you want to go. You'll design what you have to do to build a bridge between today and tomorrow. If you don't, you can never really look at your business objectively.

That's my one piece of advice. Most people think this is something that can only be done by an MBA so it's useless for them and too complex; but even a simple plan can be effective! There's a quote from a world-renowned architect by the name of I. M. Pay, "You must simplify, you must make the complex simple, and then you must make it work."

There's a lot coming at people these days—what they should do and products being launched. Day spa and salon owners are constantly being told by manufacturers, "If you'll do this you'll make more money," and, "If you do that you'll be more successful." People get confused. This refers back to the advice of creating a simple plan that will enable you to focus your time and attention and precious resources on your business in those areas that need attention goes back to marketing, of course. Do that and you'll be successful.

Wright

So what does it really take to be successful?

Finkelstein

It takes three things. It takes what I would call pig-headed determination— you just have to go at it and you have to want it really bad. It takes personal leadership, which means making a personal commitment. And it takes a vision because without a vision you don't know where you're going—if you arrive there, you wouldn't know it.

This may sound a little far-fetched and a little New Age, but it also takes a spirit that's connected to something more important than just ourselves in this world. It's a realization that we are interconnected to a Higher Being. I don't want to get too spiritual here, but it takes "getting out of ourselves" sometimes and being able to look at things beyond our own selfish interests.

Wright

Like every other business.

Finkelstein

It *is* like every other business! You have to know your business, you have to know your products, you have to know the features and benefits, certainly to the client purchasing those products and using them—it's just solid business. Everyone likes to think that their business is particularly different, certainly the quality of the people who come into the industry; but you have to understand that we're not talking from a demographic perspective—the people who are the owners and managers of these businesses *don't* have Harvard MBAs. They are people who perhaps weren't star students in high school, but most of them as owners and managers have a passion for helping people. The basic principle of these people is that they are very passionate about what they do in helping others, and the principle that applies to them is the same principle that applies to all businesses. The people in our industry are best served when they can clearly see that, and then use tried and true marketing principles to help those better serve clients so that they can fulfill their vision and their mission.

Wright

Many salon and day spa owners "work behind the chair" and feel that their work is part of their creative expression. Is there any conflict for them to be good at business as well as good at their art?

Finkelstein

No, I don't think there's a conflict. The thing is that it really doesn't matter what I think—it matters what *they* think. It's really about a mindset here, it's what you want—you can have a very successful business and still do what you like to do. If you like to do hair or if you like to be a massage therapist and if you love doing that with people, by all means put steps in place that will allow you to do that.

I met with someone the other night who is the president of TSA, which is the salon association, a part of the Professional Beauty Association. This man runs three very successful businesses that are expanding, and yet he spends time behind the chair. He even does shampoos in his business. He greets customers at the desk; he loves to do those things. So if you can figure out how to manage your time, which is a skill set that is one of the eight key strategies, then you can put systems in place that allow you to run a successful business. And do the thing you really love to do.

Wright

I've seen spas in hotel chains and cruise lines. How is it possible for a small business to compete with national chains and manufacturer-sponsored businesses?

Finkelstein

Let's go back and talk a moment about the absolute necessity for a business plan. By creating a plan you'll discover who you are in the marketplace, where your leverage points are, and what you have to do to maximize your strengths. And we go back to differentiation here, because you have to differentiate from the chains and those manufacturer-sponsored businesses.

How do you differentiate? You do that by being darn sure that you're the best local business possible. On a global front, you can never compete with the chains, but in any one marketplace you can beat the pants off of any chain! You really can, any day of the week. You know your market better than they do, you are there and you can execute better—many times you're physically present—and a chain has managers who may have very good training programs and all that, but there's nothing like having an owner who has a true interest in the success of that local business. If you learn your market and know your customers, and you put in tried and true "guerilla marketing principles," you have an advantage! It doesn't have to be anything fancy—you don't have to spend a fortune to have a very effective marketing program. You can communicate with your customers on a much more intimate level and do it more frequently. As marketers we know that frequency is necessary in order to maintain loyalty. The chains and the manufacturers basically have one way of doing things, and it's a fairly inflexible.

It's funny, I once ran one of these chains, and when someone breaks out of the fold of the chain of command so to speak, and puts in something innovative, instead of latching onto the innovation the chains are very slow to respond. They are slow to adopt something new and get it implemented in all the stores. They usually cast the person who suggested the innovation aside—the person is fired. The person is not because he or she is not doing a good job, it's because the chain can't tolerate someone working outside their chain of command or outside their methodology.

As a local owner you can be much more responsive to your clients' needs and the changes in the marketplace. And having said that, you should embrace all the disciplines—the marketing discipline, the financial discipline, the leadership discipline, and the management discipline—that the chains *do* have. You have to incorporate that into your own skill set. That's your challenge as the owner. Can you do it? Of course you can! Can you compete on price? No, don't even try. If you try to become the low-cost provider, the chains will kill you because they have a very different cost structure than the independents.

In any marketplace in any town across this country, the leading salon or day spa in the community is *not* a chain. Any individual business can not only fend off the chains, but also experience wild success!

Wright

You're right. I look at the town I am living in now and the market leader is someone who is an owner-operator. We have a lot of chain stores here, but the ones doing better business are the owner-operators who are local.

So how do you specifically help salons and day spas become successful?

Finkelstein

You know David, many salon and day spa owners are overwhelmed with all the work they have to do to build a successful business. Many times they feel the business is running them rather than the other way around, so the result is that they get all stressed about money and the challenges we talked about like finding and keeping good, dedicated professionals, attracting new clients, and finding the time that's needed while still having a balance in their lives.

So that's where I come in. I help the owners and the managers get more clients and more profitable business through my programs and products and services. I train and coach and support the people in the eight key areas of management, including the marketing area.

Each of these areas is proven to give owners more profits, more productivity, and more organization. And in the end, what they get is peace of mind about money, and they get more time to concentrate and develop what's really important. They achieve balance and they get renewed passion and new energy for their life and their business!

I help them get truly focused on those things that are important. I help them put in good ideas, and help them hone in and focus on the great things. I help them through coaching and through training to execute on these ideas. That's how I help them—I train, coach, and support them.

Wright

What a great conversation! I appreciate the time you've spent talking with me. It looks like you have a very, very interesting business and you know a lot about what you are doing!

Finkelstein

Thank you, David, I appreciate that, I really do.

About the Author

ANDREW R. FINKELSTEIN, whose family founded, owned, and operated an international chain of hair salons, literally "grew up" in the beauty business. He is a noted industry speaker, author, and business coach who specializes in salon and day spa marketing.

Since earning a B.S. in Economics from The Wharton School of Business, he has spent over twenty-five years working in every aspect of the beauty industry. He has headed up marketing, operations, merchandising, and retailing divisions, as well as owning and operating his own salon, following a family tradition that has endured for over seventy-five years.

Andrew has had the privilege of personally working with many salon industry notables and their teams on business development including Frederic Fekkai, Garren, Jean Louis David, Kenneth, Oribe, Cutler, New York's award-winning Salon AKS, and the late Noel deCaprio.

As a contributing writer to *Business Strategies Magazine,* Andrew writes the "New Leader" column. He also is contributing columnist to *Beauty Store Business.*

Currently, Andrew is putting his experience to use running The Beauty Resource, a business he founded to train, coach, and develop people in the industry using a success system that is guaranteed to get results. "There is nothing I'd rather do," Andrew says, "than work with salon and spa owners and managers, helping them to build better businesses, make more money, and live the life they've always dreamed about."

Andrew R. Finkelstein
The Beauty Resource
15 East 91st Street
New York, New York 10128
Phone: 212.831.2421 ext. 202
E-mail: Andrew@thebeautyresouce.com
www.thebeautyresource.com